Missionary & Millionaire: Transforming Cultures as Priests and Kings has captured the heart and message of Jesus in a way that will capture your heart. The author of this book is a spiritual daughter, friend, and apostolic leader whom I have walked with and counseled over the years. I have had the honor of watching her discover her identity and fulfill her destiny. A courageous life is not stumbled upon; it is cultivated. Living the life you were meant to live is an invitation for every Kingdom son and daughter of God, and Leanne clearly communicates that in this read.

—DR. LEIF HETLAND
President and Founder of Global Mission Awareness
Author of 12 books, including *Called to Reign* and *The Love Awakening*

As a member of our global apostolic network, Harvest International Ministry, Leanne Goff has impacted thousands upon thousands of lives as she walks in her God-given calling. She understands what I like to call "prosperity with a purpose," and she lives it out by stewarding the resources and influence that God gives her to advance His Kingdom. And by the grace of God, I have seen personal breakthrough and transformation in my own life thanks to Leanne's willingness to embrace the fullness of her calling as a marketplace apostle. God wants to bless you—abundantly, radically, exponentially. I believe this book, *Missionary & Millionaire: Transforming Cultures as Priests and Kings*, will help unlock faith in you to experience more of those supernatural blessings. Get ready because your life won't be the same!

—DR. CHÉ AHN
Senior Pastor, Harvest Rock Church, Pasadena, CA
President, Harvest International Ministry
International Chancellor, Wagner University

Leanne Goff's book *Missionary & Millionaire: Transforming Cultures as Priests and Kings* is an inspiring and thought-provoking testimony of a life surrendered to the Lord. So often, believers desire to be touched by God, but it is when we discover our true identity that we leave behind the pauper's poverty mentality and enter the promised land of princehood. In this book, Leanne vulnerably shares her story of transformation and gives practical tools that will help you overcome limited mindsets that hinder you from stepping into the fullness of your royal identity as a child of the King. I highly recommend *Missionary & Millionaire: Transforming Cultures as Priests and Kings* to anyone who is desiring to live in greater depths of their identity and to discover their heavenly assignment.

—KRIS VALLOTTON
Senior Associate Leader, Bethel Church, Redding, CA
Co-founder of Bethel School of Supernatural Ministry
Author of fifteen books, including *The Supernatural Ways of Royalty*,
Spirtual Intelligence, and *Uprising*

I believe so many Christians are starting to understand that to do what we are called to do, we need to have the right resources and mindset. Leanne Goff has created a book that is going to do just that—bring you into a wealth mindset but also create faith for all you are destined for. *Missionary & Millionaire: Transforming Cultures as Priests and Kings* is going to give you some very rich principles based on Leanne's own life story, and not only will you love her, but I believe she has a gift to help you to grow rapidly. I highly recommend this book for people who are looking to see God transform the world but need the resources to partner with that vision.

—SHAWN BOLZ
Author, TV Host, Podcaster, Minister

Growing up with Leanne as my amazing mom, I have witnessed her faithfulness and gratitude on display daily. Quite often people who are not in your inner circle imagine that you become who you are overnight. They rarely get to peek into the life challenges and work that you put in to becoming who you are. In this book, you are put into my mom's life to see how she was molded into the amazing mother and woman of God she is today, functioning in both a priestly and a kingly role. Every chapter has an amazing story behind it that allows you to peek into the life of my mother, friend, mission worker, and most importantly, daughter of God. As you dive into these stories, you will see practical ways of growing different parts of your life that will allow you to have a greater impact on others around you spiritually and financially!

—JEFF GOFF
Licensed real estate agent
The BC Team, Compass RE

I have known Leanne for more than sixteen years as a spiritual mom. In many of the accounts she talks about in this book, I have had the opportunity to not only to be a spectator but to also experience them alongside her. This book is a transition manual on how to use the keys of the Kingdom in your life, ministry, business, and more. I can assure you that this message is going to offend, push, stretch, and empower you to become free from the opinions of people and from an orphan and slave mentality. As a Cuban, I know very clear and near—I can say this message is going to revolutionize you! Spiritual principles will be revealed to you on how to be a king and not just how to live from earth to heaven but from heaven to earth.

—JOSUÉ SANTIAGO
Senior Pastor, Family of Faith Community Church
President and Founder, Josué Santiago Ministries

I have been a witness to much of the journey this book traces. I have known Leanne and her family for thirty years. She is not only like family to me, but her daughter also married my brother, intertwining our families. I share that only to say I can verify the transformation contained within the pages of her story. I have watched Leanne and Ray over the decades as they faithfully labored in ministry, at times living hand to mouth. I have also watched over the last few years as Leanne was transformed not only spiritually but also physically and financially. Read this remarkable book and let it inspire you to live you!

—DAVE OLSON
Senior Leader, Heartland Church

Attention all Kingdom-advancing warriors: read this book! My heart is so stirred for this powerful book from our dear friend, missionary, author, and CEO, Leanne Goff. This book is a compass to freedom and Kingdom vision. In this book, you will learn what Jesus meant in Matthew 16:19—"I will give unto thee the keys of the kingdom of heaven: and whatsoever thou shalt bind on earth shall be bound in heaven: and whatsoever thou shalt loose on earth shall be loosed in heaven" (KJV). God is awakening the mantle of priest and king (see 1 Peter 2:9) in those who are ready to lead in the Great Commission. This book is a *right-now* download from heaven. Get ready for a new mandate for Father!

—PAT SCHATZLINE
Author, Evangelist, and CEO,
Remnant Ministries International

This is a masterpiece. A masterpiece on faith. A masterpiece on resilience. A masterpiece of knowing the Father's heart. I believe what Leanne has allowed God to use her for in the writing of this book will set many people free from fear. It breaks down the poverty mindset and expresses true creativity. It shows that when you walk in your purpose, God has no alternative than to pour His blessings and favor upon you. I was humbled to be in Malaysia with Leanne when she was already filled with the Spirit. She was hungry to get more, and though lying on the floor, she reached out to someone she hardly knew because of what he carried. The more people who follow this example and chase after "the more" of God, the more the world will be transformed. Don't buy one copy. Buy as many as you can to get in the hands of people you know. It will bless them. I am very proud of my friend.

—HUGH MARQUIS
Author of *Take Your Framework and Stick It Up Your Pipeline: Finding a New Normal in Business*

MISSIONARY & MILLIONAIRE

TRANSFORMING CULTURES AS PRIESTS AND KINGS

LEANNE GOFF

Table of Contents

Acknowledgments

To the priests and kings in my life:

First my Lord and Savior, Jesus Christ, who not only demonstrated to me what a Priest and King looks like and how they function, but how to be *a little girl with a big Dad* when I didn't know anyone who was effectively living out that identity.

Leif Hetland, who has taught me how to navigate the rhythm of heaven when it comes to ministry and business— *businesstry*. I have been practicing this rhythm for three-and-a-half years now and am growing better and better at it.

Papa Jack Taylor, my spiritual grandfather, who received his upgrade to heaven in April 2021. Papa Jack understood the Kingdom of God better than anyone I know. He loved like a priest and knew how to live like a king, reigning and ruling with all authority. There is no longer a veil between heaven and him, and he now sees things clearly. If I could be granted anything this side of heaven, it would be to sit with Papa Jack for one hour and have him share with me what living as priests and kings really looks like.

To my spiritual brother, Paul Yadao. Paul and his wife, Ahlmira, had to travel their own journey, learning how to function not just as religious priests but also as powerful kings, shifting the culture in twenty-three Asian nations.

Willie Santiago, my beloved friend in Cuba, was living as a king when all of us priests thought he was crazy. But he wasn't. Eighteen years ago, Willie was thinking as a business-man in Cuba when it was illegal to do so. As a result, he has established some very successful businesses from his priestly heart that are impacting Cuba for the Kingdom of God.

Pat Schatzline was the first minister I ever heard preach a message on priests and kings: "Restoring the Priestly Kings." I was hooked on a message I just couldn't shake, and thus this book. Thank you, Pat, for awakening a book in me that was never on my dream list but nonetheless is a dream being ful-filled.

Foreword

"The harvest is among the poor, but transformation takes place through kings." C. Peter Wagner, my spiritual father and mentor, wrote those words to describe the impact that Christians are called to have in our world. The harvest—when lost souls come to salvation in Jesus Christ—is something that most of the church is familiar with. Many believers recognize the importance of placing the Great Commission (see Matthew 28:18-20) at the center of our lives and ministries. But kingship and transformation? Those are things that require a definite paradigm shift.

As we know, geopolitical leaders, including actual monarchs, have great responsibility to steward their authority and transform society for good. But there is a deeper truth in Peter Wagner's words.

The Word of God tells us that *all believers* are kings and priests before God (see Revelation 1:6; 5:10; 1 Peter 2:9). According to scripture, there is no difference between the "minister" behind the pulpit and the marketplace leader behind the CEO's desk. I believe that when the church community and the business community come together in unity, we are going to see an explosion of revival. Now is the time, in this momentous chapter in history, for us to acknowledge our royal assignments to be Kingdom ambassadors and agents of transformation.

In this book, my good friend Leanne Goff offers an exciting invitation to join her on her transformational journey with Jesus. With honesty and humility, Leanne illustrates principles of Kingdom living by telling her story and imparting biblical truth that will refresh your spiritual senses. Most characteristically, she carries a heart of honor and leads a life of integrity, reflecting the heart of the Father.

As a member of our global apostolic network, Harvest International Ministry, Leanne has impacted thousands upon thousands of lives as she walks in her God-given calling. She understands what I like to call "prosperity with a purpose," and she lives it out by stewarding the resources and influence God gives her to advance His Kingdom. And, by the grace of God, I have seen personal breakthrough and transformation in my own life thanks to Leanne's willingness to embrace the fullness of her calling as a marketplace apostle.

God wants to bless you—abundantly, radically, exponentially. I believe this book will help unlock faith in you to experience more of those supernatural blessings. Get ready because your life won't be the same!

Dr. Ché Ahn
Senior Pastor, Harvest Rock Church, Pasadena
President, Harvest International Ministry
International Chancellor, Wagner University

Preface

Missionary & *Millionaire: Transforming Cultures as Priests and Kings* has captured the heart and message of Jesus in a way that will capture your heart. The author of this book is a spiritual daughter, friend, and apostolic leader whom I have walked with and counseled over the years. I have had the honor of watching her discover her identity and fulfill her destiny. A courageous life is not stumbled upon; it is cultivated. Living the life you were meant to live is an invitation for every Kingdom son and daughter of God, and Leanne clearly communicates that.

Sixteen years ago, Leanne, and her husband, Ray, came into my life. For almost six years, Leanne operated as our executive director, as well as my personal assistant, while Ray was my resource director for Global Mission Awareness. Leanne came with a heart of a priest, missionary, minister, servant, and woman of God in pursuit of His heart. I could easily impress you with Leanne's life and ministry by sharing the sacrifices and statistics of what a laid-down lover of Jesus looks like. I have seen her go through unimaginable pain and hardship and still come out on the other side as an overcomer.

As a spiritual father, it has been a great honor to see this spiritual orphan find her way home and discover Jesus the High Priest and King in her daughtership and now be influencing and discipling nations, as well as impacting a business of more than 45,000 people. I often tell Leanne, "You have one of the largest churches I know."

This book is a must-read for anyone who thinks big, dreams wildly, and knows there is still a missing piece to experiencing God's complete fullness in life. There is a remarriage of the priestly and kingly anointing taking place in the Kingdom of God, and Leanne's book gives you a road map to a journey of accomplishing that. The silent divorce of the two has affected the body of Christ in such a way that we have been more influenced by the world than we have been the influencers.

For me personally, as a son, husband, father, CEO, missionary, and minister, I have discovered that there is a lamb and a lion in every person. Jesus, the Priest, King, and Prophet, wants you to know your true identity, experience transformation, fulfill your divine purpose, and live a life of abundance in business and ministry. This book is a journey written by a guide you can trust to help you encounter the life you were meant to live!

Dr. Leif Hetland
President and Founder of Global Mission Awareness
Author of 12 books, including *Called to Reign* and *The Love Awakening*

Introduction

You are a chosen generation, a royal priesthood, a holy nation,
His own special people, that you may proclaim the praises of
Him who called you out of darkness into His marvelous light.
1 PETER 2:9

Like many Christians, I grew up with two basic misunderstandings about how the church is supposed to work. One
was that the work of ministry is divided into those who actually do the work—professional and volunteer ministers—and
those in the marketplace who support them financially. The
other was that financial lack was just part of the sacrifice of
serving God. The people in the marketplace who supported
ministry often had a lot of money, but hardly anyone actually
serving God on "the front lines" did, and that was normal and
natural. Like Jesus and the disciples, we were devoted to more
spiritual things.

Of course, even though certain biblical verses can be used
to support these misunderstandings, they are not at all the true

biblical picture. My husband, Ray, and I found that out over time as God led us into greater understanding—and greater abundance. It took a fairly big paradigm shift to start seeing ministry in a new way, without the clear divisions we've often placed between ministry and the marketplace. We've come to see all of life as ministry, and we've learned that our Father—the King of the universe, whose resources are unlimited—is interested in establishing His Kingdom in every sector of society. And He is very creative in how He does that and the people He uses. We've learned that He doesn't divide and categorize His work in the ways His people have often believed.

This book describes that journey from one mindset to the other and from a place of lack to a place of abundance—not getting rich but creating wealth (see Deuteronomy 8:18). It includes other ministers' stories and gives examples from my own life, but the truths in it can be applied to anyone's. This is not just for people who have worked in the context that I have as a missionary and pastor with an apostolic function. It's for teachers, evangelists, prophets, worship leaders, Sunday school teachers, nursery workers—as well as business-people, lawyers, construction workers, administrators, politicians, plumbers, and everyone else who is a son or daughter of God and wants to learn how to step into a life of greater fruitfulness and abundance.

It's for everyone who is longing to fulfill their assignment and walk in their destiny for the Kingdom of God.

I talk a lot about priests and kings in this book. By that, I don't mean literal priests and kings as the dictionary would define them. I mean two sides of our calling. Sons and daughters of God have been called into both a priestly role and a kingly role—a royal priesthood, as scripture calls it (see 1 Peter 2:9).

Priests are called to represent God to human beings and human beings to God. Every believer has that calling. But every believer is also a child of the King, called to influence society at every level. We are royalty. We are destined to rule and reign with God, with authority in our world today and for all eternity. Historically, the church has majored on the priestly role but often missed out on our royal assignment. That's the side we need to grow into.

Living out our kingly assignment does not mean leaving behind our priestly functions. Those are still absolutely essential. But we can continue to fulfill our priestly roles while also stepping into the realms of kings. Priests bring God's wisdom, power, and love into human situations, but they rarely transform the culture. Kings—leaders in government, business, and society's institutions—are the ones positioned to transform society.

If we need a good model for that, we only need to look to Jesus, who was and is both Priest and King. He knew how to interact with people in high places and leaders in the marketplace, as well as with religious leaders and common people. We are called into that broad kind of influence too. Priesthood and kingship are very much a part of everything we do.

You can be a king regardless of whatever your God-given assignment is. You may worship and encounter God inside the four walls of a church, but you represent the King outside of them. In one way or another, you are called to be an influencer representing the Kingdom of God.

I hope you will catch a vision for how to do that in the pages that follow. Though much of this book tells the story of how we learned to see God, ministry, and provision in an entirely new way, it's much more than a story. It is filled with truths and teachings God has shown us every step of the way. I encourage you to take those truths and teachings and apply them to your own life. You will be amazed at how God leads you and provides for you as both a king and a priest to represent Him well, influence the world around you, and see His Kingdom coming for you, in you, and through you.

1

A New Identity, a New Way of Thinking

All I ever wanted to do was be a missionary. Every time a missionary came to our Baptist church in Kenner, Louisiana, I'd sit on the front pew and listen to their stories. I was glued to their slide presentations. I loved the scenes from marketplaces and orphanages around the world. Each time the speakers clicked their projector from one slide to the next, I almost felt like I was there. And I hoped one day I would be.

Ray and I took our first trip to Honduras in 1982 and loved it. We got bit by the mission bug and infected with the mission virus. We returned from that trip trying to figure out how to go into mission work full time. We took other short-term trips and eventually trained with Youth With A Mission (YWAM) in Lindale, Texas. We spent two and a half years with YWAM in the U.S. and ministering in Guatemala. Then we spent ten years with Teen Challenge in the U.S., leading periodic mission teams from Teen Challenge to Mexico.

So when we were offered the opportunity to move to Mexico in 2002, we took it. We resigned our positions with Teen Challenge and moved south. We were on the mission field! And I loved being there.[1]

It did not go as expected. We had some challenges and setbacks in that season of my life, and, frankly, I was not in a place to manage them well. After five months, we returned to the U.S. I was devastated, to say the least. In all of that effort over the years to serve God as a missionary, I had been striving. I was busy trying to do His will and save the world, working hard from a heart full of insecurities, fears, disappointments, and a need to be somebody significant in His Kingdom. It was more than I—or anyone—could handle.

I was living *for* God rather than living *from* Him. Instead of resting, I was wrestling.

> " We were on the mission field! And I loved being there. "

When we returned from Mexico in 2002, I felt like I'd failed God. My whole dream had gone up in smoke. I had gotten to the mission field, and it felt amazing to be there, but then it fell apart. I felt like I had missed my opportunity. I wondered if God would ever use me again. I know that sounds crazy, but that's the way someone with an orphan mindset thinks.

---

[1] I tell the story of our journey into missions in more detail in my book *A Christian Life Without Father God* (2012).

When we came back to the U.S., we didn't know where to live. Our two main choices were Iowa, where our daughter lived with her husband and children, or Tennessee, where our son lived. We chose Iowa. While I loved being near our grandkids, it wasn't the mission field I dreamed of. Being in Iowa or anywhere else in the U.S. felt like a death sentence. I spiraled downward, deeper and deeper into a major depression.

I felt like God had given up on me. And I felt like I was giving up on everyone and everything.

I worked for an insurance company for a few months. I sat in a cubicle punching about 40,000 keystrokes of prescriptions every day. It was a job, but it wasn't what I was created to do.

I loved God, and I loved serving Him. But I was in unfamiliar territory, like I'd been cut off from the vision He had given me for my life. I had been to revivals all over the world—Dr. David Yonggi Cho's church in South Korea when I was newly married, the Brownsville Revival many times during our season with Teen Challenge, and many places where God was doing amazing things. But I was a desperate woman wondering where He was.

As a new resident in Iowa and with winter setting in, I felt a cloud of depression hovering over me. My doctor suggested antidepressants to help me manage the condition I found myself in. I was desperate for a breakthrough, so I thought, *Why not?* There were many times at my job I'd go to the bathroom and stand in the stall and cry. *God, what did I do wrong? Are you punishing me?* I felt abandoned.

I wasn't thinking like a daughter of God. I was living in a paralyzed condition with the perspective of an orphan.

Before our brief term in Mexico, our son-in-law, a worship pastor, knew of a revival happening in Toronto. Sometimes he would send me DVDs of people like Randy Clark and Heidi Baker ministering there. Even though I'd been to revivals before and had great experiences at them, I really had no desire to go to Toronto. I had prideful, orphan thoughts—*Been there, done that. Why do I need it?*

So there I was, still depressed and desperate. One day, I got down on our living room floor and cried out to God. "Something has to change," I said. "I know you didn't create me to live this way. I don't care anymore about my reputation, my ministry, my credentials, or any titles. I lay them all down before you."

It was the prayer of a desperate, hurting heart. I felt something began to shift, as if that moment was a major turning point in my life.

When I found out our church was taking its first team to the revival in Toronto—known then as "The Father's Blessing"—I was one of the first to sign up. I remember telling my pastor that even though I knew Jesus as Savior and friend and felt very close to Him, I had a hard time seeing God as my Father. I knew He was—that's a basic biblical truth that believers everywhere just accept as true and right. But *my* Father? He just didn't feel that personal.

That's because I viewed God through the lenses of my biological father, who was not present in my life and always kept his distance. He was completely detached. I knew that non-relationship was affecting my view of God, but I didn't know how to change it. I couldn't overcome the feeling of God being a distant, detached Father. This is a common issue for orphans when they have an adopted father but are struggling with the idea of how much that father loves them. It's just as true for many Christians who see themselves as spiritual orphans. We know God is our Father, but we don't always feel fathered. And we don't know how to get that head knowledge into the depths of our hearts.

So I sensed that God was someone who just tolerated me rather than celebrated me. If I needed something from Him, I'd go straight to my brother, Jesus. God would answer Him because He was His *Son*.

I didn't know what to expect by going to a revival known as "The Father's Blessing," but somehow I thought God might be attracted to my desperate heart.

We arrived late the night before the conference started. The first session was scheduled at 2 the next day. Since Niagara Falls was only about an hour away, our group decided to fit in a trip to the falls. But as we were getting into the van, our son-in-law and I decided we didn't want to go. We hadn't come to Toronto for sightseeing. I needed a touch from God! Like the woman who had to press through the crowds and touch the hem of Jesus' garment to get a touch from Him, I was desperate for Him. I didn't want to miss a thing—even if it happened while the people at the conference were still preparing for the thousands of people who were about to converge on the auditorium.

As soon as I walked into the church, I sensed a love I had never known before. I sat there for four hours before the first session. I just sat and waited. I listened to the worship team warming up and watched people come in and out as chairs were being set up. I soaked it all in.

About four thousand people from all over the world were coming to the event. Everyone received a lanyard in one of four colors so we could rotate sitting up front. People with blue lanyards sat in the front the first day, orange the next, and so on. We were in the back on the first day, so that's where I camped out while I waited.

Finally our group came back as the first session started, and after a time of worship, the conference leaders welcomed people from different countries. "Where are our people from Australia? From England? From the Netherlands?" There were people from almost everywhere, so it was a long list. Then they asked for "our family in Mexico."

Our pastor turned to me and said, "Don't you wish you were them?"

"Yes," I said, frustrated. "I'd rather be with them than with you!" He knew what I had been going through. He understood what I meant.

John Arnott, the lead pastor at Toronto, then invited all the Mexicans to come down to the front to receive prayer. Then he said, "And if you speak Spanish, I want you to come down."

I thought, *Wow, they're going to pray for people who speak Spanish.* I knew some words, but it was very broken Spanish. Still, that little bit was enough for me. I went to the front and found myself with a bunch of dark-skinned, dark-haired people with their hands out to receive prayer. I'm sure the ministry team wondered why I was there among all those Hispanics.

Later, I found out what John Arnott really said: "If you speak Spanish, I want you to come down *and pray for them.*" I guess God didn't want me to hear the last part. He had set me up. He knew I was desperate for even a hint of an invitation. I heard what I needed to hear to get me up front with them.

My pastor later told me, "Leanne, you stole the birthright."

While I was up there, hungry to receive a touch from God, somebody on the prayer team came along and said, "More, Lord!" I hit the ground and was down for two and a half hours, glued to the floor and crying like a baby. I couldn't move my arms or open my eyes. I felt God's love moving in and out of me the entire time. This started before the preaching, which I'm sure was great, but I didn't hear any of it. When I opened my eyes two and a half hours later, I saw about another hundred people plastered on the floor like I was. Everyone else had gone to dinner.

After I got up and went to the restroom to clean up my face from all the crying, I sat back down in the empty auditorium and asked, "God, what happened?"

The encounter I had with Him over that two and a half hours is indescribable. But what He said transformed my life. "Leanne, you've been a woman of virtue, a woman of passion, a woman with a heart after me, and a woman of God. But I don't want a woman of God anymore. I want a little girl who knows she has a big Dad." Needless to say, I was shaken!

> " But I don't want a woman of God anymore.
> I want a little girl who knows she has a big Dad. "

I had always prioritized being a woman of God so He would be able to use me. But a little girl with a big Dad? I'd just never thought of Him—or myself—that way.

But there was still one big problem: I didn't know how to become that little girl. I had to figure out how to walk out what He desired. I knew a slew of pastors, evangelists, worship leaders, ministers, and missionaries. But I didn't know anyone who was fully living their life with God as a true son or daughter of His.

So I asked Jesus to teach me how to be God's daughter. He knew how to be a son; surely He could teach me how to be a daughter with a big Dad! That's when everything seemed to shift. I didn't walk the same anymore. I didn't talk the same anymore. I didn't think the same anymore. I didn't live the same anymore.

—— BECOMING A SPIRITUAL DAUGHTER ——

I had learned about Randy Clark and his ministry Global Awakening, which included a network called the Apostolic Network of Global Awakening (ANGA). I wasn't sure what the role of an apostle looked like, but I was anxious to learn. I took part in a ministry trip Randy was hosting to China in June 2006, and on that trip I learned of a minister named Leif Hetland and how passionate he was about Cuba. That caught my attention because I had been to Cuba a few times over the last couple of years.

Since my experience in Toronto, I had grown my own ministry during that season—Missionaries In Action (MIA)—that hosted teams going to various nations. We were based in Iowa and associated with a church there. I had a great board of directors and several missionaries working with me. In addition to hosting teams, we took care of missionaries by processing their support, handling their newsletters, praying for them, and freeing them up to do what God had called them to do. And part of what we did took me to Cuba. That nation captured my heart so strongly that I asked God in March 2006 to give it to me as an inheritance, during our first pastors' conference there in Cardenas.

In October of that year, I was being ordained by Randy's network at his Voice of the Apostles conference and discovered that Leif Hetland was going to be ordained the same time I was. So when Leif was introduced at our network meeting, I made it a point to go to him during one of the breaks and introduce myself.

"My name is Leanne Goff," I told him, "and I understand you go to Cuba."

"Yes, I go there often," he said.

"I've been going there for quite a while too."

"Let's talk," he replied.

On the last day of the event, we connected again. I got to know Leif over the next few months, and he was able to put words to my experience in Toronto. As I shared the encounter I had, he told me, "Leanne, you had a baptism of love."

I had always heard of a baptism of water, a baptism of repentance, and a baptism of fire, but I'd never heard of a baptism of love. This is actually the core of Leif's teaching, and he expresses it so beautifully. After three years wondering how to describe what had happened to me on the floor at that conference, I finally had a language for it.

A few months later, Leif and I partnered our teams on a trip to Cuba. I watched him for the first couple of days running around trying to get a rental car, take care of all the little details, and drive people around. Here was the leader of a world-renowned ministry trying to handle everything himself.

"Don't you have someone to help with all this?" I asked.

"No, I don't," he said. He had an office assistant back home, but he didn't have anyone to assist with his logistics and travel details.

"I'm going to pray that God will send you someone."

Little did I know that I was praying myself into that position. I had no thought of handling that responsibility. I was the founder and president of my own ministry in Iowa. I traveled to places like Mozambique and Mexico, in addition to Cuba. I was not envisioning myself as an assistant to another ministry.

A few months after that Cuba trip, the license Leif had from the U.S. government to go to Cuba expired. His office assistant had also resigned. "Why don't Ray and I come down to help you for a week?" I suggested. I had done the application for my license to Cuba for years, and I figured we could help with that and a few other administrative items.

So Ray and I took a trip to Alabama, where Leif's ministry was located at the time. While we were there, everything seemed to fit. Within a few weeks, we were moving from Iowa to Alabama—just for a year to help him and his wife, Jennifer.

Near the end of that year of working with Leif and Jennifer, I took my first trip to Pakistan with Leif. Leif is very particular about who he takes to Pakistan because of the unique assignment he has for ministering to hard-to-reach groups and high levels of leadership there. He doesn't open his Pakistan trips to just anyone who wants to participate. It's by invitation only. So it really was a great honor to be a part of that team.

I'd already traveled to about thirty nations, but that trip to Pakistan was like no other I had been to. It had a major impact on my life.

It's very difficult to communicate that kind of experience to someone who has never been to that country. It's like asking an astronaut to describe what going to the moon is like. There just aren't any words for it. Pakistanis seem to never sleep. They pray five times a day, starting at 5 in the morning. Honor is very highly valued in Muslim culture, though it's not always a Kingdom honor. The women are literally behind a veil, covered from head to toe in a 130-degree heat index. We Westerners find it hard to get up and go to church on Sunday mornings, yet Pakistanis would literally die for what they believe. It all boggled my mind. It really is hard to describe.

On our way back to the U.S., we stopped for a couple of days in Dubai for a break. It was during Ramadan, so no restaurants were open except in hotels. For breakfast, our team went down to the hotel restaurant where the tourists had gathered to eat. Leif and I were sitting across the table from each other when he surprised me with a question.

"Where do you stand within the GMA family?" he asked. Global Mission Awareness is the name of his ministry, and everyone associated with it is "family." Actually, Leif sees the entire Kingdom of God as family. He doesn't have "conferences"; they're "Family Meetings." But in this moment, he wanted to know where I fit within the "family" of his ministry.

"What do you mean, 'where do I stand'?" I asked. I had no clue what he was talking about.

"Where do you see yourself?"

"Well, I'm your personal assistant. Your administrator." I didn't know what else to say.

"I want to father you," he said.

Leif is about ten years younger than me, but he has a father's heart. He has many spiritual sons and daughters around the world. I'd seen how two of them, Paul and Ahlmira Yadao from the Philippines, wrote emails to "Daddy Leif," and I thought that sounded kind of strange.

I told him, "I'm not ready to call you Daddy Leif!"

I never knew my biological father, but with my baptism of love four years earlier in Toronto, I knew God was my Father. And I was perfectly fine with that. I had come to a place where He wasn't just God anymore; He was *my* Father—a Father to this fatherless one. I honestly didn't think I needed a human father anymore.

But when Leif asked that question, I started crying, picked up my purse, stood up, and said, "Can we talk about this somewhere in private?"

"No, we can talk right here."

I believe we have different chambers in our hearts: one for God; one for our biological father, mother, siblings, spouse, and children; and chambers for others who are in covenant relationship with us. I was 50, and that chamber for my father—not God as my Father, but an earthly, flesh-and-blood father—had never been opened by a human being. That day, Leif reached across the table, pried it open, and started rummaging through it. And it hurt.

Over the next few months, I felt like I wanted to die. I wanted to get plastered or go dig a hole in our backyard and bury myself. I was in so much pain.

I'd go to the office and cry. I didn't wear any makeup for weeks because I'd just cry it off. I would come home and make dinner for Ray and me, and afterward I'd light some candles, put on some music, get in our Jacuzzi, and just cry.

I would cry out to my Father in heaven, *Why do I need a spiritual father? I have you! You're enough! I don't need anyone else!* I couldn't understand what was happening because I kept trying to figure it out with my mind instead of my heart.

Our one-year commitment to Leif and Jennifer ended that following December, but God was doing something new in my heart, and we knew we had to stay.

> " Why do I need a spiritual father? I have you!
> You're enough! I don't need anyone else! "

The following February, Leif was diagnosed with a tumor in his abdomen. We weren't sure if it was malignant or not. People around the world began standing in the gap for him. As he went into surgery, the doctors were concerned he'd come out with a colostomy. Thankfully, the tumor was benign, and no colostomy was needed. But Leif had several weeks of recovery, which meant no traveling or ministry.

We canceled most of Leif's ministry commitments, but for a couple of them, he flew in his spiritual son Paul Yadao from the Philippines. I accompanied Paul on one of the trips to Iowa. On the first day he was speaking to about twelve ministry leaders in a small setting, and after lunch he had us take time to be still before God and "know Him."

I found myself on the floor during that session. As I lay still, I sensed something like a beam of light coming out of heaven, even though I was facedown. God spoke to me and said, "My daughter, I put Leif in your life to father you."

"You did?" I started crying.

Paul didn't know what was going on, but he came over, knelt next to me, put his arms around me, and embraced me. As he did, it felt like a lightning bolt went through him and into me. We were both overcome by the power of God.

"Paul, I can call him Daddy Leif," I said.

Paul was aware of my struggle with that language. I didn't get it, but at that moment it got me! When we get something, it changes us. But when something gets us, it transforms us. Here I was, four years after the Toronto encounter, going through another level of transformation.

After that experience, I fully let Leif into my life as my spiritual father, and I'm so thankful I did. Our one year of serving him turned into more than five. If I had to choose between restoring my relationship with my biological father or having Leif serve as a father to me, I'd choose Leif—hands down. I can't help but call him "Daddy Leif" now.

——— THE MIND OF A KING'S DAUGHTER ———

The next season of my life was a period of continued, massive transformation. My thoughts began to shift in many ways. I went to a new level of thinking—from the perspective of an orphan to thinking like a daughter, learning to be that little girl with a really big Dad. I began to learn how to serve not only in a priestly role but also in a kingly role, establishing the Kingdom in every area of my life. And with that royal identity, my entire perspective on finances began to shift. I went from having a perspective of scarcity or lack to seeing a reality of fullness and abundance.

With every one of those shifts, the circumstances of my life have changed dramatically as well. When God is going to transform the situations in our lives, He begins by transforming the way we think, see, and hear. An inner breakthrough always comes before an outward breakthrough. I have seen that happen again and again, and every time it does, I've found myself in radically different situations than the ones I was in before. God was overhauling my life in answer to things I had prayed many years before but didn't know how to enter into.

One of those radical transformations was in my view of money. During our missionary years, we had the idea that less was best. The church has historically given the message that having little is holier than having a lot, and I had certainly bought into that way of thinking. The poorer we were and the more sacrifices we made, the more we felt like we were suffering and sacrificing for Jesus. That was our "missionary" mindset.

This mindset played out in many different ways in our mission experiences. When we lived in Mexico and Guatemala, people sent care packages with treats in them. We'd give our kids a ration of two Oreos a day. I probably need to ask their forgiveness. But we saw treats like that as rare, special privileges.

Someone in Texas gave us a Jeep when we were on the field. The floorboard had a few holes in it, and our kids could see the road passing underneath them. That whole picture of "just getting by" or making unusual sacrifices made us feel like we were really suffering for Jesus the way we should.

Financial austerity is appropriate in certain seasons in our lives—people do make huge sacrifices to follow and serve God, and that's important. Paul wrote about being content in humble circumstances, and we absolutely need to be willing to do that (see Philippians 4:12). Many of us go through lean times, especially when we're starting out as adults, when we learn how to economize and steward the money God has given us. That's part of how He teaches us.

But this idea that the only way to follow and serve God is by suffering and depriving ourselves of any financial comfort is wrong. Paul told the Philippians that he also knew how to live in plenty, to abound (see 4:12). He was comfortable with scarcity, as many believers who serve God are, and he was comfortable with plenty—a much more challenging concept for people in ministry. We need to know how to live in all circumstances, whether with little or a lot. And I believe God wants His people in most seasons of life to have an abundance of resources to advance His Kingdom.

Ray and I knew from the start that we weren't called to the typical American lifestyle of working all day just to survive or save up a little and then get up the next morning to do it all over again. I've always known we were created to disciple nations. That's our calling. But we thought that rejecting the typical American treadmill could only mean being worse off financially for the sake of Jesus.

Over the last few years, my mind has been completely reoriented to a new way of thinking regarding finances and abundance. Anytime God does something new in our lives, challenges and tests come. I've been seeing finances from a whole different point of view. God has prepared me over that time to steward money not to get by on as little as possible but to build Kingdom wealth for His purposes. And part of that preparation involved testing me in order to trust me with what He eventually wanted to bless us with.

> ❝ Anytime God does something new in our lives, challenges and tests come. ❞

2

Seasons of Testing

My mindset about finances—and many other things—really started to shift when we met Leif. He started flipping our thinking right side up. I studied him. I watched how he treated people, how he handled finances, and how he blessed people spiritually, materially, and every way he could.

I saw people stab Leif in the back and then watched how he dealt with it. It might take him a few days to process it, but within a very short time, depending on how deep the wound was, he would turn around and be willing to wash that person's feet. He could kiss their cheek with no malice in his heart at all. I studied how he did relationships and how he always showed up for his Kingdom assignment, no matter what was going on.

I saw how Leif handled finances. He had money, but money didn't have him. He would freely bless people with whatever God had given him. In most of the church, even among pastors and other ministers, money has them—even if they don't have very much of it. They are bound to it, always chasing it, trying to get more of it either to survive or thrive. Because I'd never had a relationship with an earthly father, I'd ask Leif questions about how to do this or that, or what to think about the things that came up in our lives, including everything about finances. It was a time of radical reorientation in the way we thought.

In that whole season, God was turning our minds around in so many different ways. I had always lived from earth to heaven, from a place of lack trying to pull down whatever I needed from a place of abundance. I never realized I could live from heaven to earth, and rest in that place of abundance, believing God for the supply of whatever I needed on earth. I wasn't sure exactly what that looked like, but I learned by watching Leif. God was teaching us a lot.

As I mentioned, our year with Leif turned into five and a half years, and during that time I saw many "hope to be" sons and daughters come and go. Many didn't pass the tests. They always wondered why they couldn't sit at the front row of the conference or get to go to the green room to meet whatever VIP happened to be there that session. They had the same orphan mentality that I had had for so long. There was always some comparison—"Why does he get to go? What about me?"—and they just didn't last. They weren't thinking like the sons or daughters they were.

Most tests were unintentional, but some were not. To prepare for the African Call of 2008 in Tanzania, right before my first trip to Pakistan with Leif, I went two weeks early to help put the event together. I had a lot of experience leading teams, and we were expecting people from all over the world. We had people at three hotels and five conference locations and would be getting around on five buses, so a lot was going on. I was there to help coordinate all of that.

Finally, the big event came, and on the last day, we were at the foot of Mount Kilimanjaro with about 10,000 Africans there to worship. It lasted the whole day, and I had to make sure everything was moving as it should. Leif and I met with all the speakers the night before to talk about the agenda for the day, as well as how we were going to take up an offering. We would take the buckets we used for washing the feet of widows and orphans in the morning and put them on the edge of the platform so people could have an opportunity to give. The money was not coming back to GMA, of course, but staying in the country for ministry there. We had it all planned out.

I was on the agenda to speak that afternoon, releasing a blessing over the women present. Someone else was to follow me to speak a blessing over the men. Right before we did that, Leif said, "I want you to do the offering."

"Me?" I responded. "I'm speaking, and I have to make sure everything's running smoothly. Can we get someone else?"

"No, I want you to do it."

When it was my time to get up, I was trying to figure out how to minister to 10,000 people, half of whom were women. As I asked God how to minister to the women, He told me to bring them all to the front, so I did. Then He told me to have them partner with one another. "You're going to pull heaven down, and they're going to be the ministers for each other."

So I spoke for fifteen minutes about bringing heaven to earth, and then I told them to partner up, put their hands in the air, and on the count of three pull heaven down over their partner. By the time I got to "three," heaven came down. There was a whirlwind with dust clouds on the edge of the crowd, and God's presence was palpable. I was left standing there thinking, *What just happened?* I was absolutely stunned.

Leif was standing to the left of me at the far edge of the stage. I motioned to him.

"You want me to take the offering now?"

"No, not now."

I walked over and gave Leif the microphone. "This was a test, wasn't it?" I asked.

"Yes, it was!" He smiled and gave me a big hug.

So I passed the test. And more tests, some intentional and many more that were not, continued to come as my mindset was shifting in so many different areas. When change comes, it gets challenged, and I was changing radically. I was learning to see God, myself, our ministry, and our finances in entirely new ways.

> " When change comes, it gets challenged,
> and I was changing radically. "

—— THE TEST OF LOVE ——

Sometime around December each year, I ask God, "What's your word for me next year?"

The word for 2011 was, "I'm going to test you on how well you love."

I was being fathered by someone known as the ambassador of love, so that's what I wanted as my inheritance—not Leif's anointing but his capacity for love, which always astonishes me. I had my baptism of love in 2002, and for several years, I had watched how well Leif loved. I observed how he lived it out, never letting anything distract him from the calling to love supernaturally. And like him, I wanted to love God well, love myself well, and love others well. God told me He was going to test me in each of those ways.

I wasn't a bad person before my baptism of love. Not at all. I served God the best way I knew how. But like many evangelicals, I was very focused on working for God rather than working from Him—all about doing, getting things right myself instead of letting His power work through me. I was still saved and going to heaven, of course, and I loved God as well as I could—at least as well as someone can love a Father they see as distant and detached. But I became a different person after that experience in Toronto. And by spending several years working with Leif, I learned the difference between being an evangelical and having a Spirit-filled life.

So 2011 was a year of love tests, which were really tests of whether I was seeing God, myself, and others through the lenses of heaven. If those lenses are clouded, you can't see or love God the way He really is, and that's what had caused me in the past to live like an orphan—like I always needed to look out for myself, guard my heart against disappointment, and assume that living in scarcity was what I deserved.

When you have that distorted view of God, it doesn't matter if you're a son or daughter. You still live like an orphan. I had always felt like a failure and thought I was stupid and ugly and would never amount to anything—hallmarks of an orphan mentality. God changed my view of Him in that baptism of love, but it took some time to learn to live like a little girl with a big Dad.

Toward the end of that year, I got on a plane in Atlanta to go to Cuba. I hurried onto the plane, sat down in business class, and heard, "You passed the test."

Lord, what do you mean? I thought.

"You've passed the test of love. You've loved me, you've loved yourself, and you've loved others well."

Wow, I thought. I was really encouraged to hear that.

"Next year, I'm going to test you on your faith. How strong is it?" That was my word for 2012. Oh, hallelujah... another test!

THE TEST OF FAITH

That March, the day after my birthday, I was in Houston for a conference and got word that my mother had had an accident. She had fallen and fractured her femur. The accident itself hadn't caused her death, but her immobility caused pneumonia to set into her lungs. Within three weeks, she got her upgrade to heaven.

That happened amid another severe trial we were going through. Our assistant, Sonia, was at fault in a serious accident and was facing up to forty years in prison. That's not what ended up happening—God orchestrated a miraculous story of rescue, redemption, and restoration for all involved—but in the midst of everything going on, we weren't sure how it was going to turn out. It looked impossible.

While she was facing that horrible situation, Leif began moving his offices from Alabama to Georgia. We had been planning that for a year. But Sonia couldn't leave the state, and she didn't know anyone in Alabama because she had only been there a very short time. On top of that, Sonia was challenged with multiple sclerosis, with fourteen lesions on her brain and spine. What would we do with her? We couldn't just leave her behind to go through her trial alone. It was a real dilemma. Miraculously, at the last minute the judge let her go with us.

One thing after another that year stretched and tested our faith. But we got to the end of the year, and God said, "You passed the test."

"Thank you." I breathed a sigh of relief.

——— THE TEST OF FINANCES ———

In December 2012, God spoke again. "I'm bringing another test to you. This year, it's the test of finances." That was my word for the entire year—the third year in a row I'd be tested for something specific.

In March of that year, I was speaking in a church in north Atlanta when I heard God say to start a church in that area. I had been preaching about God's presence from 1 Samuel 3, and when we're still in His presence, He'll stand in ours, as He did with Samuel. Even as I preached, I sensed such a stillness and rest in His presence. As I was ministering to people at the end, God spoke to me and said, "I'm going to demonstrate to you what you just preached. I want you to start a church in north Atlanta."

" When we're still in His presence, He'll stand in ours. "

"Whoa, Lord," I said. "I don't want a church. I'm not a pastor." But I was convinced He had spoken to me.

As we were driving back to the south side of Atlanta where we lived and Leif had his office, I kept thinking how crazy this sounded. I didn't know what it meant. Me, start a church? It just seemed so unexpected. The next day, I went into Leif's office and said I needed to talk to him. I told him all about what had happened the night before.

"I think it's God," he said.

I had already been in a process of transitioning out of being his assistant. I knew the time had come. I loved doing that for him, and I'd do it all over again with joy. But after five and a half years of being his assistant and executive administrator, it felt like the oil and breath for that assignment were gone.

I'd learned that it isn't a sin to lose the vision for something you've been doing, but it's a sin to stay when you've lost it.

I still had a vision for being Leif's spiritual daughter and serving him any way I could, but it would have to be in a different capacity. In fact, I had been asking him for months to bless me and release me, and he kept saying no. He didn't think it was quite time. I know I could have left anyway, but I didn't want to go without his blessing. Eventually, though, he said yes, and I agreed to stay on to train my successor so the transition would be smooth for his ministry. I was in no hurry to leave because I didn't know what God was preparing for me.

So when God spoke to me about the church, I already knew I would be doing something else soon. I just didn't know it would be that. But it was clear. God gave me a vision for the church, a name for it, the next steps, and everything. When we started it in July 2013—the Atlanta HUB (His Unlimited Blessings)—God just rolled everything out for me, even the leadership team. It was clearly His work. But it was also a huge step of faith financially.

We planned our first service for a Saturday. On Friday, I got a text from someone I didn't know.

"Hi, Leanne. I'm a specialty nurse, and I have a patient who is dying of cancer. I wanted to know if you would come pray for him."

Something she said, although I'm not sure now what it was, gave me the impression that this patient was somehow involved in leading worship. But it was a text conversation, so there weren't many details.

"I'm launching a church tomorrow," I texted. "There's a lot going on. Maybe I could come Sunday afternoon?"

"I'll be at the service," she replied. "I've heard you preach, and I'll come tomorrow night."

We decided that I would go pray for her patient at 4 on Sunday afternoon.

Leif spoke at the Saturday night service. Afterward we arranged a "love tunnel" for people to come through so we could lay hands on them, speak the Father's heart over them, and release His love into their lives. While we were blasting people with love, a woman came through the tunnel.

"You're coming to my house tomorrow?"

"Oh, is it your husband I'm coming to pray for? What's your name?"

She said her name was Nancy and her husband's name was Jim. I told her I was honored to be asked to pray for Jim and would see her tomorrow.

When Sonia and I went to their house the next day, it was not at all what we expected. They lived in a huge mansion, and just to get into the community I thought we were going to have to give blood. (Obviously not, but it was all *very* impressive.) The house was gorgeous. I must have misheard the nurse; I didn't know how a worship leader could live in a house like that. It was beyond description.

The nurse came out to greet us, led us into this insanely beautiful mansion, and took us to a large breakfast area to introduce us to Nancy, her daughter and two sons, and an assistant. Sonia and I sat and talked with them for almost four hours in that huge room. We got to know them and told a lot of stories that would build up their faith for a miracle. We shared about kneecaps being replaced in the Philippines, Sonia being healed of multiple sclerosis—she had fourteen lesions on her brain and spine, right in the middle of her legal trouble, and her MRI showed that she was totally healed—and many other testimonies of God's ability to heal. We just did life with them for a few hours. And the whole time, Sonia and I were thinking, *Who are these people?*

Finally I asked, "Are we ready to pray for Jim?"

They said yes and took us out on a veranda overlooking a golf course. Jim was at the opposite end of it, outside their bedroom. He was propped up on something resembling a hospital bed, essentially in a comatose state. I got on one side, Sonia got on the other, and I noticed that God's presence seemed really strong. I realized the nurse must have been praying for him consistently.

We prayed, declared healing in Jim's body, decreed that there would be no cancer in him—everything we knew to pray. We were done after about thirty minutes, and Nancy walked with us out to the car. She thanked us, hugged us, and we said our goodbyes. As we pulled out of the driveway toward the street, I turned to Sonia and said, "This is not about a man getting healed of cancer. This is a test!"

In that moment, I realized I didn't want anything from Nancy. She was extremely wealthy. We had just started a new church and were therefore in need of finances, yet I had no urge to try to get anything from her. I still had no idea who she and her husband were. I just wanted to love her and her family well.

When I arrived home, I pulled out my laptop and looked them up. To my surprise they were at the very top of a huge company, leading the company in sales for years. They had homes all over the world and their own private jet. They were very well known—and obviously living in great abundance.

I soon got a text from Nancy saying that Jim's numbers were dropping, so I texted back and told her we were praying and asked her to please keep us updated. Then I texted Leif— he was away, ministering in Alabama at the time—and asked him to call me as soon as he could.

Leif called about twenty minutes later, and I told him about the situation and asked him to pray.

"Ask them if they want me to go pray for him tomorrow," he said.

"I don't need to ask. They'll want you to go."

I called Nancy to tell her Leif was going to their home the next day to pray for Jim. She had heard him speak on Saturday night, so she agreed right away. When Leif got there, he spent three hours praying with them. Nancy's brother, who had been deaf for years and wearing hearing aids, was instantly healed. God clearly showed up. It was an amazing experience. But Jim didn't improve.

About a week later, I was preparing to fly out and speak at a women's event in South Dakota and got a text from Nancy.

"Leanne, Jim died."

I felt like I'd been gut-punched. I'd seen miraculous healings all over the world, but it didn't happen with Jim. I didn't know what to say.

I called Nancy. "I'm so sorry," I told her. We chatted for a while, and then I took off for my conference. She and I texted while I was traveling, and I found out that John Maxwell was their neighbor, friend, and pastor. He would be leading the memorial service. It was streamed live, and I was able to watch it from South Dakota. But even on the morning of her husband's memorial service, Nancy was texting me early to say that she was praying for me and believed I was going to greatly bless the women at the conference. I could hardly believe she had just lost her husband of forty years yet was praying for me, but I knew it was because we knew how to honor one another.

Three weeks later, Nancy attended a Jesus Culture conference and called to say she wanted to buy tickets for Sonia and me to go. She had never been in a service like that before. She's a strong believer but at the time wasn't as familiar with the supernatural. "You've got to come," she said. "I feel like they're talking about you."

So Sonia and I canceled our other plans and went, along with several other people she had invited. We ate at a nearby restaurant during a break, enjoying just hanging out for a while and talking about the conference. When Sonia got up to get us some coffee, Nancy followed and stood in line with her.

"I want to do for her what you do. How can I take care of Leanne?" Nancy said. "Money will never be an issue. How can I take care of her?"

31

Sonia knew my heart. "Nancy, Leanne just wants relation-ship," she said.

"Oh, she already has that!" Nancy assured her.

I found out about this conversation on our way back to the event because Sonia and I were alone in my car. I'd never asked Nancy for anything because I knew this was all about the relationship, not finances. I even knew after studying Leif all those years that this was some kind of test—a major one. And I knew that when we don't pass our tests, we have to go through them again. This one was about finances because they are very important to God—how we steward our finances and choose to love people without some sort of hook or an ulterior motive to get something out of them. And to be honest, that wasn't a temptation with Nancy. I wanted to love and honor her well. She's an amazing woman.

The only time I ever received anything from Nancy was when I was raising money for Cuba after a major hurricane had devastated the east end of the island. I had put out an urgent bulletin through my ministry for others to come along-side the Cuban people, who were in desperate need of assistance. Nancy contributed toward the need. But other than that, I just enjoyed being around her, going to her home, teaching her family how to soak in God's presence, and honoring her however I could.

That was maybe my biggest test of finances, but there were others—not because I didn't pass but because God confirms our new perspectives by giving us opportunities to practice them. The second test came when a man at our church wanted us to meet a wealthy friend, a retired engineer who had received a lot of money as an inheritance from someone who wanted him to steward it for the Kingdom. It seemed like a good relationship to cultivate. We were pioneering this church, and this guy was in a position to help.

So this man came to our house, and we sat there for while just listening to his stories. He's a lay minister with a powerful anointing for healing and plenty of testimonies to share. We loved listening to him. After about an hour, he asked, "What can I do for you?"

I sensed that God didn't want us to ask for money, so we didn't. Instead, one of Leif's spiritual sons came to mind. Todd was truly like a brother to me. He was battling cancer in Seattle and was getting close to death.

"Actually, I need you to pray for my spiritual brother," I said, and I told him about the situation.

We needed money. Pioneering a church is hard, and it's costly. But I knew that wasn't why this man was in our life. So I asked him to pray healing for Todd.

"Okay," he said. This humble man with a powerful healing anointing asked if I had a handkerchief, so I went and got one. He anointed it with oil, we prayed over it, and Ray set it aside so we could mail it to Todd. Then we talked to this man for a while longer.

A little later, he asked again. "What can I do for you?"

"Nothing," I told him. I still felt like God didn't want us to ask him for anything. Among everything else I learned from Leif, I knew not to miss the tests. Nothing was wrong with this man's money; he had gotten it honestly and his intentions were good. But God was testing my heart.

"Thank you so much for your time today," I told him. "And thank you for praying for Todd. This was amazing."

Our new friend headed home, and I never saw him again.

The third test was in Cuba in 2013. Leif had come along to join our team, bringing a few millionaires with him. We had a very fruitful trip. It was a blast, and while we were there, one of the millionaires later invited us to come stay at his house in Florida for a few days. I checked with Leif—I learned to honor him in the connections he made for us—and accepted the invitation. We had a wonderful time in this man's beautiful home and out on his boat. But we never asked him for anything. It was 100 percent about relationship and honor.

In fact, all relationships are about honor. If we're going to learn to steward Kingdom finances well, we need to remain focused on relationships and not what we can get out of them. My life verse is Matthew 6:33— "Seek first the kingdom of God and His righteousness, and all these things shall be added to you"—because I learned many years ago that if we make God our priority, our focus, He'll take care of everything else. There are two parts to that verse—His Kingdom and His righteousness—which means making Him our priority and doing whatever He tells us to do. And seeking His Kingdom and His righteousness always involves loving people without an agenda and honoring them with Kingdom honor.

God may provide for us through the people He connects us with, but the goal isn't provision. It's to build the relationship for the sake of the relationship, to love without a hook. And after these three tests in 2013, I knew I could do that.

And God knew I could now be trusted.

3

An Unexpected Breakthrough

If you can win the heart of a king, you can shift a culture. Just ask Joseph, Daniel, or Esther. It's not just about having influence or making the right decisions. If you want to have impact on a society and transform the way things are done, you need to be able to influence the influencers, and the way to do that is to love them without a hook. Like Joseph, Daniel, and Esther, you learn to live with a heart and spirit of honor.

> " If you want to have impact on a society and transform the way things are done, you need to be able to influence the influencers. "

I found myself in that type of situation when I was called to pastor a church in Ohio. Honestly, I was not interested in moving to Ohio. We were living in north Atlanta, where I was pastoring our church. I loved living in the Atlanta area. I love warmer weather. I love the South. I loved being close to a major international airport and the simplicity of jumping on a plane and going to another country with ease. But God had a new assignment for me.

The church in Ohio is a great church with wonderful people, but they needed a culture shift. It had been in existence for fifty-three years, and I was to be the third pastor since its founding. They had never gone through an interview process for a pastor, so this was new for them, especially the elders. The previous pastor of thirty-two years had succeeded the founding pastor. There were 160 applicants for the position, and I was one of them. My name was thrown in the hat following a conference I had done at the church the previous year. The interview process took approximately six months, after which I was selected as their new pastor.

I preached my first message as their new pastor in August 2013. Two weeks later, I found myself sitting in a board room with ten elders, all men. I could hear their thoughts loud and clear: *We have a new pastor, and she's a woman. How do we do this?* The testosterone was soaring around the room. Thankfully, I was raised with five men in our home—my stepfather and my four brothers. I knew I needed to win their hearts before any healthy decision-making was going to take place.

The name of the church is Family of Faith Community Church, and things were not going as well there as they once had. The congregation had been around 700 people at one point, but they were down to around 100 when we arrived.

They once had a strong network of cell groups, but now there were none. There was no women's or men's ministry—not much going on that enabled them to "do life" together. And I was all about doing life with people.

There were many issues we as a board of elders needed to work through, and we did. I didn't go in like a bull in a china store and start blowing things up. I knew that approach wouldn't help. But winning their hearts would, and that's what I did!

One issue we had to deal with was the parking lot. It was horrific—more than twenty years old, full of cracks and potholes. The elders and I were very concerned that someone, especially one of our many seniors, would fall and hurt themselves. So this issue was front and center for us.

When we first arrived at the church, a few members told me, "Pastor, we're praying for a millionaire to come and pave our parking lot."

"No, we won't do that," I'd tell them. "First, a millionaire won't step within ten feet of our property if you have a hook. If a millionaire pays for paving our parking lot, that's great. But it will be a greater testimony to our community if *we* pay to have that parking lot paved ourselves." Our only goal in that community was to love and honor people without an agenda.

About two and a half years later, we spent $160,000 to pave that parking lot. Over that time, the minds of the congregation shifted not only on the issue of finances but also on their sense of identity and views of family—things they wanted and needed but didn't know how to enter into them. I had an apostolic calling, beyond just a pastoral role, to change the environment and help them see themselves and their community from heaven's perspective.

When I was selected as their pastor, Leif suggested I read Samuel Chand's book *Cracking Your Church's Culture Code*. Samuel speaks of honor in that book. He tells a story of honoring the past with a time capsule while moving into a new era. Our congregation consisted of many people who had been at the church for years and loved it. They had prayed, sweated, and labored for a new season and for an impact on the community for God's Kingdom. I wanted to make sure we honored the past while embracing a new culture shift and future.

For five weeks, we had the congregation bring pictures of significant events in the life of the church—weddings, baby dedications, celebrations, or anything else they wanted to bring that would honor the church's past. We had a lot of seniors in the congregation, so they had a lot of great memories to include. After each service, people would bring their photos up, and we stapled them to the platform wall—a large area. We then put new sheetrock over that wall, preserving it for later generations, creating a time capsule. We were honoring the past while embracing the future. It was another way to win the hearts of the people as their new pastor. Family of Faith went from a surviving culture to a thriving culture.

———— A PROMISE OF BLESSING ————

Ray and I were doing fine financially during those years at FFCC. We weren't living paycheck to paycheck. Ray had a good job, and I received a sufficient income from pastoring. In addition, I was also a volunteer law enforcement chaplain for our county. At that time, the state of Ohio had the highest number of overdose deaths from fentanyl and carfentanil in the entire country—eleven to fourteen per day.

Also in that season, due to an adrenal crash I had in 2010 in which I almost died, I put on thirty-five pounds. I didn't know anything about those little glands that sit on top of each kidney, but I'm just about an expert on them now. Our adrenal glands produce many important hormones, and when that crash hit, my hormones got whacked out, and I started to gain weight like never before. I went from a size 8 to pushing a size 14. I was also popping antacids every night before bed like they were candy due to terrible acid reflux. My joints, especially in my hands, ached terribly, so I frequently downed joint-pain meds.

Needless to say, I was completely miserable. I would wear larger shirts on Sunday morning when I'd preach to cover up the fat I was gaining. I didn't like how I felt, how I looked in the mirror, or how my clothes fit. I got sick often. I knew something had to change, but I didn't know how to make the change.

I was on another team Leif took to Pakistan in May 2017. On the way there, we had a stopover in Dubai. God spoke to me there: "Leanne, I have an assignment on your life. You have to get hold of your health or you won't finish well."

"Father, I won't do a diet!" I lovingly responded. "I don't know anyone who has found a diet that has worked." I knew a lot of people who had "survived" a diet only to put the weight back on after a few months, and often they gained more weight than they had lost on the diet. (I find it interesting that the first three letters in diet spell "die"!)

66 You have to get hold of your health or you won't finish well. 99

Pastor J.R. Polhemus of The Rock Church in Castle Rock, Colorado, was with us on that trip. He's in his 70s but is very fit—works out every day and eats healthy, even when he's traveling. He takes really good care of himself. While we were in the mall in Dubai, Sonia and I were sitting on a bench and feeling like blimps, while J.R. stood behind us.

"J.R., I need an anointing to get healthy," I said. He put his hands on our heads in the middle of this mall, surrounded by Muslims, and prayed. That wasn't quite what I was looking for, but I certainly wasn't going to turn it down. One of our team members took a picture of us, which I didn't know at the time. I thanked J.R. and filed it away in my memory. I didn't think much more about it.

When we got back from Pakistan, I went through a session called "The Courts of Heaven." Two women from our church were training in this ministry. There were others who wanted to go through it, so they asked me if I'd go through it first so I'd know what they were participating in. So it was already on my schedule even before we left for Pakistan.

The Courts of Heaven is a ministry founded by Robert Henderson. He has several books about entering into the courts of heaven to make petitions for ourselves and the Kingdom of God.[1] It was new to me, and I wasn't sure what to think of it, but I knew Robert had spoken at the church in Toronto and was highly endorsed.

I went through this session, which you do with people who help guide you through it. You have to fill out papers before you go, but I couldn't identify a specific reason for petitioning the courts, so I went without a clear agenda. It was in the home of one of the women, and when I got there, I saw that it was all set up with a nice, heavenly ambience for the session. The presence of God felt very strong when I went in. I sat down, and they asked me what I was going to petition the courts for.

"I don't know," I said. "My life's pretty good except for being thirty-five pounds overweight and feeling physically miserable. Other than that, things are going well. I don't know what to ask for."

"Well, let's pray and ask the Holy Spirit what you should petition for," they said.

So we prayed, and soon several things came up:

---

[1] For more information on the courts of heaven, see http://www.roberthenderson.org.

- My health because I wanted to be able to finish my race well
- Our finances because I wanted to be able to fund my own assignment for the Kingdom of God wherever I was commissioned to go and not have to rely on other people
- An inheritance that we could leave for our children
- Our church because that was my main focus of ministry at the time

So we brought all of those petitions to the courts of heaven.

It was a five-hour session, and it was indescribable! It's completely led by Holy Spirit. When they were about ready to finish, I said, "God's not done yet. There's a door He wants me to walk through."

"Okay, let's go after it," they said.

I closed my eyes, put my head down, and immediately saw myself walking up to the threshold of a door. When I opened the door, I saw a room that was split down the middle. One side was illuminated by light, the other totally dark. Both sides had four doors, but I couldn't see those on the darkened side. I just knew in my spirit they were there. I explained the room to the team and told them about the four doors on the bright side.

"Go ahead," they said. "Open them."

I opened the first door and saw beautiful green hills as far as the eye could see. It was a gorgeous scene, with cattle, sheep, and horses covering the hills. It was so beautiful and hard to describe.

"I will give you the cattle on the hills, as far as you can see," the Lord said. "I'm going to bless you."

I went to the next door and opened it. Inside, there were crowns and jewels—amazingly beautiful rings, sparkling necklaces, and lavish treasures, something like you'd see in an Indiana Jones movie. Again, the Lord said He would bless me.

Then I opened the third door, and what I saw inside was like a large lottery placard that says how much the winner has won. The placard I saw had a million dollars on it.

"I will restore what the locust has eaten," the Lord said. "I will return what has been stolen from you."

I knew immediately what that meant. In my first book, *A Christian Life Without Father God*, I tell the story of how both of my inheritances were taken from me. My estranged father's wife had compelled him as he was dying to leave the minimum to my five siblings and me. He was not extremely wealthy, but we would have received a nice nest egg. Instead, I received a check for one dollar in the mail as my only inheritance from him—all he was required by the state of Mississippi to leave us. His fourth wife and her three children received his estate.

Through a misunderstanding, I also received no inheritance from my mother. The Saturday morning following her upgrade to heaven, I grabbed my Walkman and went out for a walk to process her passing. I still miss her so much. While I was out walking, I was kind of complaining to my Father:

"Father, I have no inheritance. I don't get it. Why?" I asked.

"My daughter," He said, "your inheritance is not the riches of this world. It's the nations."

"You're right," I admitted. "I'd actually rather have the nations than riches any day." I repented for complaining, kept walking, and decided I was fine. I forgave those I needed to forgive and moved on.

A few days later, when I was in the office, I heard God's voice. "I'm going to bless you with riches too."

"What? What do you mean?"

"Because of the way you handled that disappointment, I'm going to bless you with riches in this world too."

That was in March 2012. Fast-forwarding to May 2017, as I was going into the courts of heaven, I opened a door and saw a million dollars on a sign. I knew it meant God was ready to fulfill that promise from five years before.

Before I even got to the fourth door, I knew what was behind it and started crying. Our son and daughter-in-law (and daughter-in-love) had miscarried when they were pregnant with triplets eight years earlier. On the day we heard the news that they were expecting triplets, God told me they were like Abraham, Isaac, and Jacob, the fathers of nations and generations. It was heartbreaking when they were miscarried.

When I opened the door, I saw two boys and a girl, all about 8, just the age they would have been on earth. They were playing "Ring Around the Rosie," holding hands and having a wonderful time together. I broke down weeping. It was just a wonderful extra kiss from Papa God to let me see our grandchildren. I will never forget that moment as long as I live.

I closed that fourth door and began to back out of the room. As I stood on the threshold, I turned toward the right, the dark side.

"God, what about this side?" I asked. "I know there are doors over there."

"That is for Family of Faith church and its leaders for things prior to your arrival. They will have to come and take care of those doors."

So a couple of weeks later in my church office, the two women came and went through the courts of heaven with some key leaders and intercessors from our church. They entered into the doors God had reserved for the church.

THE POWER OF A YES

A month or two later, after coming back from that trip to Pakistan and going through the Courts of Heaven, I saw several friends on Facebook from our church in Iowa, whom we had known for years, melting away and looking great. I had discipled some of them, and each of them had joined me on a mission trip to Mexico or Cuba. I knew them well and knew the health history of all the women. Now they looked amazing!

What are they doing? I wondered. Whatever it was, I wanted to know. I wanted to look the way they looked.

I flew from Ohio to Iowa that following July to see our daughter, son-in-love, and grandkids. While I was there, I connected with some of these old friends, mainly to discuss a women's ministry event I was planning. We sat in a coffee shop and talked about that for a while, but when we were done, I looked across the table and spoke directly.

"I don't know what you've done to look the way you look, but I want to look like you." I didn't say I wanted to diet or lose weight. I wanted to *look* like them because they looked fantastic. And let's face it, we women like to look nice.

They told me about a health program that they had not only participated in but had become coaches for. They explained how they got involved and how the whole program worked—that it had a weight-loss component but was more about overall health.

I immediately told them I wanted to do the program. I also said, "I don't know how much you make as a health coach with your company—if it's $50 a month. But everyone on the planet needs to look like you! So I want to become a coach too."

I knew I needed to go home and get Ray's blessing, but he knew how miserable I had been feeling, and of course he was all for it. I really didn't have any extra bandwidth in my life to take on something new, but I had a strong conviction about this. So I became a client and a coach at the same time.

At the time, I didn't know what the program would do for me. I just saw it as something I needed. And it worked wonderfully! I lost thirty-five pounds in a few short months. I dropped back down to a size 8. I haven't taken any antacids, joint-pain medication, or anti-inflammatories since then. *And* I reset my metabolism at age 61. The only downside to our health program is that you need to buy new clothes. Ha ha!

I often teach on the power of our yes, and my yes that day in 2017 has now had a positive impact on the health of more than 45,000 people and on the financial wellbeing of more than 2,200 coaches. God was setting us up for a tremendous blessing.

Sonia was my first client. She was in Texas visiting family that July when I started. When she came back, she kept teasing me about my "space food." A couple of weeks into my new health journey, she decided she wanted to try my space food. She got on the program, lost fifty-three pounds, and dropped her cholesterol by forty points. Ray got on it too and lost thirty pounds, and his doctor took him off his blood-pressure medication. We all saw amazing results and still do.

A few months later, that picture of J.R. laying his hands on Sonia and me in Dubai resurfaced. I had completely forgotten about it. But God was definitely answering that prayer.

It wasn't long before people at church were seeing me transform right before their eyes. They started saying, "Pastor, you look great!"

"I feel great!" I told them. I actually felt years younger than I was.

"You look amazing, Leanne!" many others were saying. "What are you doing?"

I would explain everything and encourage them to do the program and become a coach too. I had no trouble assuring them it would transform their lives, and it just kept spreading from there. People who had never walked through the doors of our church were emailing and asking about the health program we were doing at Family of Faith. I didn't make an extra effort to promote it. It just got out there by word of mouth and living out loud. It grew organically. God's oil and breath were all over it.

Within nine months, finances were coming into our bank account from coaching others to optimal health. I didn't even know specifically how much; I wasn't keeping close tabs on it. One of the ways God prepared us for what was coming was by leading me to hand our finances over to Ray years earlier. He would be better at it, and I didn't need to be distracted by it. So I wasn't on top of all the details. I tell people now that I was like Jacob. God wrestled me to the ground and said, "I'm going to bless you." I got up with a limp and haven't walked the same since.

He blessed us with the health program, He grew our business, and He continues to bless a tremendous number of people through it.

He was fulfilling extravagant promises He had made long ago because He knew I was ready to handle them and steward the financial increase well.

4

A Season of Acceleration

In September 2017, Leif told me his ministry was doing a conference—a family event—in Malaysia, and he'd like me to be there. I was already scheduled for trips to Sri Lanka and Cuba, so we worked it into our travels, which ended up including seven nations and seventeen airplanes in sixteen days.

When we got to Malaysia, I was sitting on the front row during one of the services. Leif had already spoken, and he came over at one point to pray for me. I felt God's power and immediately went down on the ground. As Leif continued to pray for me, two other people came over—a saxophonist who prophetically played his music over me, and another man, Hugh Marquis, I had never met but had heard about. He was an entrepreneur from Australia with a strong business anointing. Somehow, even from my position on the floor, where everything kind of seemed like a blur, I knew it was him standing there next to me.

By this time, even though our business was barely just beginning, I knew my Father had given us a business and wanted to bless it. I had always had somewhat of an entrepreneurial spirit, even though some of my ideas had never gotten off the ground. I had been reading some books by Gary Keesee, who teaches ministers to have four streams of income, and I was bothered that we didn't have that yet. Ministers rarely have an inheritance to leave for their children and grandchildren because for most it's not a particularly profitable career financially. So in my awareness that this businessman was standing next to me while I was being prayed for, I grabbed the leg of his pants at his ankle and thought, *I'm going to get every bit of business anointing you can impart to me.* I said nothing out loud; this was just what I was consciously pulling on. As long as he was there, I was going to go for it.

> Ministers rarely have an inheritance to leave for their children and grandchildren.

I've talked to this man since then, and we've laughed about me trying to steal his birthright. But I believe I really did receive an anointing for business from him that day. A lot of things that had happened—the testing I had gone through, J.R. laying hands on us and praying, going into the courts of heaven, and pulling on that entrepreneurial anointing—had led me to a place of extraordinary blessing.

─── PUTTING THE RIGHT PLATES ON THE TABLE ───

I had a handful of clients within a couple of months. Sonia was the first coach to sign on with me. Ray joined me a couple of years later—though he was always 100 percent supportive—once he was able to fit it around his job. In November, Sonia and I went to hear Leif speak at a church near us in Ohio and spent some time with him after the service.

I was making a few hundred dollars a month at that point, but I still wasn't very aware of how it was happening. Whenever people told me they wanted to do the program, I would sign them up and coach them. Whenever I needed to be away in Cuba, Sri Lanka, or wherever else, my mentoring coaches in Iowa would offer to take care of my clients and the coaches I was mentoring while I was away. The business grew, even when I was out of the country.

While we were talking with Leif, he mentioned how healthy Sonia and I looked. Together, we had lost 88 pounds since the last time he saw us in Malaysia. He asked what was going on, and I explained the health program we had gone through and the business side of it. And I admitted that with pastoring and being an author, helping oversee 350 churches in Cuba, and being a law enforcement chaplain, as well as wife, mother, and grandmother, I had too much on my plate.

"No," Leif said in his fatherly way, always looking at the bigger picture. "You have too many plates on your table."

He was right. Wife, mother, grandmother, pastor, chaplain, spiritual mom, author, speaker, organizer of women's events, overseer of a network of churches across Cuba—too much was on my table. I had too many roles to do them all well. Ray had even been telling me so, yet there were reasons for each of those roles that involved contending for the Kingdom on multiple mountains of society. It was hard to let go of any of them. But now, especially with my spiritual father weighing in, it seemed like the right time.

A couple of bottles of water were sitting on the coffee table where we were talking. As Leif told me I had too many plates on the table, he made a sweeping motion with his hands as if he were wiping the table clean. He told me I needed to recognize what were priorities, the assignments for this season, and what weren't—to reprioritize all my roles and responsibilities from scratch.

Some were nonnegotiable, of course. God, my family, and my calling to the nations and our church weren't going to come off the table. But how many nations, and which ones? That was open for discussion. And my new business of health coaching—up until then, it had been a little teacup saucer on the very corner of my table, not even one of my big plates. Among all the things I was doing, God was bringing me to a new level. I needed to figure out what to say no to so I could have a big enough yes to what I should be doing. I needed to review what would serve me, my family, the church, and the nations well, and what wouldn't.

In fathering Ray and me, Leif had taught us the difference between an investment for the Kingdom of God and an expense. An expense drains us; an investment charges us. Most people *spend* their time, talent, and treasure instead of investing them. When we spend something, there's usually not much growth; but when we invest, we generally see a return—many times a great return—on our investment. We needed to determine for the next season which of our roles would be an expense of time, talent, and treasure, and which would be an investment.

We decided that my season of law enforcement chaplaincy was one of the plates that needed to come off my table in the near future. It had been a wonderful experience and important for a time, but it no longer fit on my table as a priority. A few months later, I turned my badge over to my chief chaplain. I had gone into it thinking I was just going to pray for people, but it involved a lot more than that. In fact, my first callout was a DOA. I carried a raid backpack, wore a raid jacket, and carried handcuffs and Narcan. It was quite a responsibility, and I was honored to serve our community, but that season was coming to an end.

There were some other things that I shelved for a season, not necessarily permanently, in order to give our business time and space to grow. That was one of the wisest decisions I have made. It allowed God to expand our work supernaturally in ways we could never have predicted.

That conversation with Leif had been eye-opening to me. Every month after that, Sonia would help me clear off my table again and reprioritize my assignments for the Kingdom of God. Within nine months of regular reprioritizing according to each month's demands, I apparently reached a huge milestone in the business, and I wasn't even aware of it.

Sonia and I had just returned home from our annual business convention in St. Louis. We picked Ray up and headed to dinner. We were sitting in a steakhouse, and I looked at my phone after we ordered. One of the health coaches on our team had become an executive director, and my mentoring coaches were celebrating her in a text thread. Then I looked at the next thread where I was pictured reaching first-time FIBC—a Fully Integrated Business Coach. I didn't know exactly what that meant, but I knew it was big. I started crying like a baby in the restaurant. I was clueless!

When we got home, I pulled up the compensation sheet and saw that I was earning about $6,000 a month after nine months of coaching. I thought, *Wow, if I can do that not knowing what I'm doing, what if I figure out what I'm doing and help others do it too?* So that's what I did. I went all in.

I stepped up as an entrepreneur and began managing my business as a Kingdom CEO. Before, I had just tried to manage my business as an amateur. Now I was going for pro. Within three months, I reached Global Director, which brought Ray and me a very nice income. I wanted to give the gift of our health program *and* the gift of our business away to anyone and everyone. Every person in America and beyond deserves the opportunity to have each of these amazing gifts.

Once I reached Global Director, I knew in my heart that my time serving as pastor of Family of Faith was near its end. I'd been there five and half years and raised up a strong leadership team. The church culture had shifted and was doing very well. We were ministering to the community in ways we had not done before. Several hundred people came to our food pantry every month—a ministry that had not existed prior to my arrival. We were once tolerated in our city; now we were celebrated (and still are). The leadership team's networking with other pastors was healthy and strong. Things were going well. But I knew my assignment and that season were done.

The church's board of external overseers, which included Leif, agreed that my time there was complete. We brought all the elders together one Saturday morning, and I read a letter asking for their blessing for me to transition out. I didn't just announce that I was leaving; I asked for their blessing in keeping with the culture of honor we had carefully cultivated. Most of these elders and their wives had gone through our health program, and they knew I no longer needed to be at the church for a paycheck. Money didn't take me to Ohio, and money was not going to keep me there.

"I want to give up my salary so we can hire another pastor," I told them.

"No, we still want to pay you," they said. "We want to honor you as our pastor and for what you've done here." By this time, they knew what honor looked like. But I told them I didn't need the money.

They insisted. "Whatever you decide to do with the money is up to you, but we want to honor you."

So we ended up giving it all back to the church. In fact, we still give to that extent. We now give to the Kingdom of God in one year more than double what we used to make. It's Ray and my desire for that percentage to grow each year.

" We now give to the Kingdom of God in one year more
than double what we used to make. "

The elders and I carefully navigated my transition over the next six months. During a Sunday morning service in December 2018, I preached a message called "The Power of Decision" and announced to the church family that Ray and I would be transitioning to Nashville to be closer to our son, daughter-in-love, and two grandchildren. We put all the pieces in place to make sure my departure went smoothly, both for Ray and me, and especially for the church. Three months later, we made our move to Nashville. I've been told by many, even pastors, that they've never seen a pastor go through a church transition so well with no fallouts.

My spiritual son Josué, from Cuba, whom I had known for seventeen years, had been one of our associate pastors for a few years. He was more than qualified to step into the position of senior pastor. I knew he could take the church to the next level. Before he and his beautiful wife, Leyanet, came to the United States, he was overseeing thirty-two churches in Cuba. Josué wears the mantle of pastor.

Once March came, we were all ready. Years later, Family of Faith Community Church still has a thriving culture and is doing great things for the Kingdom of God. Josué continues to lead that amazing church family as they are making a significant impact on the community and the state of Ohio.

—— AN APOSTOLIC CALLING TO GET THE CHURCH HEALTHY ——

In 2019, Ray and I reached $1 million per month in revenue. Our sponsoring coaches were celebrating us, and one of them asked, "Do you know what that means?!"

"Um, no, I have no idea," I said. A million-dollar-a-month revenue business was just a number to me.

Three months later, Sonia and I were driving back to Tennessee from our church in Ohio where I had been ministering, and as we were entering Nashville, it hit me. I turned to her and said, "I know what that means now! It means a million dollars of products are being bought through our organization every month. That's crazy!" Of course, at the moment, Sonia thought I was crazy. We both had a good laugh.

That was a huge awakening for me. It's not that I don't like numbers or know how to deal with them. I do. But I'm not money-hungry, and I just don't put that much thought into the levels and landmark moments. I know we must manage our business and do it with a spirit of excellence, and we do. We bring excellence into everything we do because that's important and honoring to the people we work with. As a result, we've reached close to $3 million a month in revenue as I'm writing this book, and our income has naturally increased along with that. I'm not constantly poring over the compensation sheets to see how that happens. It's just something I trust God for.

In April 2021, Ray and I reached another milestone of $83,333 per month in income. Most people have no idea what that number means. I didn't before I became the CEO of my Kingdom business. That number actually means millionaire results—with a monthly revenue of $2 million-plus in our business. Ray and I didn't expect to hit that milestone for another three to four months. I was actually on my way to a summit held at Ché Ahn's church, Harvest Rock, in Pasadena, when I received a text from Ray with a screenshot of our monthly bonus informing me we had reached $83,333 per month.

I was scheduled to meet with Ché while I was at the event. Not long before, he had interviewed me for his TV program about what was going on in Cuba, as well as in our country. Then the interview went in the direction of our health-coaching business. In fact, since that interview Ché and his wife, Sue, signed up for the program, love it, and have experienced incredible results from it.

While I was waiting for Ché outside his office, another gentleman was standing there too. He asked me how I got connected with Ché and what brought me to the summit we were attending.

"I'm looking to be better equipped as a marketplace minister," I told him. "I know I've been functioning as a pastor as well as a missionary. I've been a pastor for several years, but I believe I function more as an apostle."

A pastor shepherds people and makes sure they're taken care of, but an apostle functions more as a CEO, an organizer, a leader who equips others for their Kingdom assignment.

I then told the gentleman a story that had been going on for the previous few years. It went way back—I had been a part of Randy Clark's Global Awakening network for a long time, but about four or five years before this summit with Ché, while I was pastoring in Ohio, I felt there was more for me to step into on that front. I remember feeling a rumbling in my spirit about this apostolic mantle while on a drive to Atlanta. But I didn't understand it. I had been in Randy's network, Apostolic Network of Global Awakening (ANGA), for many years and had some training for that kind of assignment, but the pieces didn't fit yet. I *had* to talk to someone about it.

I'd usually talk to Leif about these sorts of things, but he was ministering in another country. So I called Papa Jack Taylor—Leif's spiritual father and a grandfather figure to me. I explained what I was feeling and my background in that area, and I asked if there was a book that could help me understand my function as an apostle.

"He's using you to write the book," Papa Jack said in his loving, convicting voice. He had a heart for encouraging people to blaze new trails.

"I don't have time to write a book, Papa," I told him respectfully. "I need a book now!"

Papa Jack offered some good advice, which I took and moved forward. About a week later, after I was back at the church, one of my spiritual daughters from Atlanta sent me a photo of the cover of one of C. Peter Wagner's books, *Apostles and Prophets*. I had never heard of it, and she had no idea what was going on with me over the last couple of weeks. I asked her where she got the book and why she sent me that cover photo, and she said, "I just came across it and thought about you."

So I ordered the book immediately and read it on the way to a conference at Bethel Church in Redding. I was consumed with it the whole way. It seemed like Peter had written that book specifically for me. It helped me begin to understand my function—not as a title or a job to put on a business card, but how to operate in the role of an apostle.

For the first time as a pastor, I felt like I was stepping out of a pair of shoes that didn't quite fit me and a coat that felt awkward and into shoes and a coat that fit me perfectly. I was beginning to understand my true function in the fivefold ministry as someone called to serve as an apostle.[1]

Several months later, after our transition to Nashville, one of our prophetic intercessors at our church in Ohio sent me a recording about the roles of apostles, prophets, and intercessors. I listened to it and got a lot out of it, but I started wondering, *Who out there was in the business of equipping apostles?* Apostles have an assignment to equip people who carry the mantle of prophet, evangelist, pastor, teacher, and everyone else in the body of Christ in order to exercise their spiritual gifts, but who was equipping the apostles? I needed more.

In an online search, I found one of Ché's books called *Modern Day Apostles,* so I ordered it. I discovered that he had a network and a School of the Apostles for equipping them. I applied and was interviewed, and when they learned of my connections with Leif, Global Awakening, and other apostolic leaders, I was accepted immediately. I went to my first

---

[1] The fivefold ministry of apostles, prophets, evangelists, pastors, and teachers is presented in Ephesians 4:11-13.

Global Summit in Pasadena in August 2020. At the time, Ché was suing the governor and state of California because of discriminatory Covid policies, and even then, it was considered an illegal meeting. The police showed up and it was a real adventure, but not foreign to me after going to Cuba, China, and Pakistan over the years.

> " The police showed up and it was a real adventure. "

Now, back at Ché's church for another summit the next year, this gentleman waiting with me outside Ché's office asked how I was connected with him. I told him much of this story of wanting for years to understand how to function in an apostolic role.

"Even though I had already been functioning that way for a while," I explained, "I'm just now grasping the reality of it." I told him how we had been in ministry for years in those priestly functions, but now with our business, we were figuring out how to function among kings. I knew very well how to live in sonship; now I wanted to learn more about apostleship in order to fully walk out my Kingdom assignment here on earth.

"What kind of business do you do?" he asked.

"I'm actually a health coach," I said, and I told him the story of how that got started and that we had just reached the monthly million-dollar revenue mark and $83,333 income mark.

"I'm with *Charisma* magazine," he told me. "I'd love to do your story."

So we exchanged names and contact information. I then realized Ray and I would be in Orlando a couple of weeks later. *Charisma* gave us first-class treatment from the minute we walked through their doors all the way through the interview. We were there for four hours as they got our entire story. It was God's timing and a wonderful experience.

Since then, several people who also have an apostolic or prophetic calling have joined our business network. One international speaker and health coach in our company is extremely passionate about the priest-king assignment. He is also in the process of writing a book about those functions and the anointing that comes with them. These people have just taken off with the health-coaching business. They've gotten healthy themselves and are also helping thousands of others do the same.

Collectively, we are on a mission to get the church healthy in spirit, soul, and body, with healthy mindsets, relationships, and finances, in addition to our lifelong focus on spiritual growth and the advancement of God's Kingdom. They all go hand in hand, like a beautiful, creative tapestry.

I believe one of the reasons we haven't completed the Great Commission is a lack of finances. I know many people who have an assignment for the Kingdom and a great passion and heart for carrying out their calling. But they are so limited because of their financial resources. It's an enormous problem we must solve.

This isn't God's problem, by the way. He owns the cattle on a thousand hills. All resources belong to Him—not wealthy nations or foreign kings, not the titans of Wall Street and Madison Avenue, but God, the King of the universe. Everything on the planet is His. So the question is, how can we tap into what He already has? How do we understand that invitation, and how do we steward the resources He has given us?

Most of us are very familiar with the saying "God won't give you more than you can handle." We generally think of it when we're going through a rough patch in life or all hell seems to be breaking loose. But I also believe the flip side. Can God trust you with a business? Can He trust you with wealth? Can He trust you with an abundance of wealth to steward for His Kingdom and the Great Commission? If He can, He will give it to you!

Ray and I have spent our past few years trying to educate ourselves on this issue and help people learn to build Kingdom wealth. We went through a season of acceleration as God kept opening doors, raising the stakes, and drawing people into our network of clients and coaches. But we believe the entire church is in a season of acceleration in stepping into new ways of thinking and experiencing new levels of power and provision. It has become clear that this is a key strategy in advancing God's Kingdom purposes.

For example, if I was doing a pastors' event in Cuba, I had to raise the thousands of dollars it would take to host that event. Just two months prior to beginning my health journey and launching our health-coaching business, I hosted two women's events in Pakistan. Those two events cost thousands of dollars that I had to raise. Now with any event God calls me to do stateside or internationally, I can fund my own Kingdom assignment.

Don't misunderstand me—there is nothing wrong with others sowing into my ministry or Kingdom assignment. People do—every day! I would not want to restrict them from receiving a blessing (see Acts 20:35). Why? Because they believe in my assignment, and they trust me. But I don't have to wait on someone else or use the excuse that I just don't have the money to do it.

Many Christians feel limited by lack of resources: *I don't have the money to take that mission trip that's been on my heart forever. I don't have the money to build that orphanage. I want to open a home for children and women caught in human trafficking, but I don't have the money.* Again, this is not God's problem. He has more than enough resources.

God said, "I've given you the ability to create wealth" (Deuteronomy 8:18). But we often skip right over Scripture passages like this. How many of us have heard a sermon on that verse? God has streets of gold and pearly gates. He owns the cattle on a thousand hills. That's *a lot* of cattle! The problem isn't a lack of resources; it's the limitations we've put on ourselves in receiving them.

──────── A MINISTRY OF BOTH/AND ────────

Heather Wallace, one of the women in our business network, has been in ministry with her husband for more than twenty years as pastors, speakers, and leaders. But not long after health coaching was introduced to them and their business began prospering, she was asked a question that made her stop and think: "When did you make the jump from ministry to business?"

It was a sincere question from someone who genuinely wanted to know, but it came from a mindset that these two areas of life were separate from each other. After reflecting on that question for a few moments, Heather offered this woman a new perspective.

"I never made a jump from ministry to business," she said. "My business is an extension of my ministry because ministry is not always what we've perceived it to be. It isn't a title or assignment or agenda. It's a calling. It's who we are at our core."

Heather went on to explain that business simply creates the profitability that we were created for as sons and daughters of God. As the Bible makes clear, we're the head and not the tail, the lender and not the borrower, above and not beneath (see Deuteronomy 28:13). We become conduits for God's Kingdom to come. The church has often believed this when it comes to healing or demonstrations of God's power and presence. So why not when it comes to finances?

Financial provision is a critical part of advancing God's Kingdom on earth, so when we become effective in both ministry and business—or actually see them as two aspects of the same work—the ministry that happens inside the walls of the church begins happening outside of them too. It's not one or the other. We've been given dominion over it all.

As a young woman coming up in ministry, Heather was taught what so many people have been trained to believe: that you can be anointed as a "priest" or as a "king"—someone in ministry or in the world of business and government—but not both. But that isn't what scripture teaches. David is a great example; he functioned as both a king and a priest at times. We've also been taught to believe that Christians, especially those in ministry, are not supposed to prosper. But John prayed for his friend Gaius that he would "prosper in all things and be in health," just as his soul prospered (3 John 1:2). How can we be the ones to take care of widows and orphans if no one among us has the financial means to do it?

"I truly believe we are supposed to rise up in this generation and take back the keys God has given us," Heather says. "He has given us all dominion, authority, and power to exercise in both the marketplace and on the mission field. We are at our best when we fully operate as both kings and priests."

> " He has given us all dominion, authority, and power to exercise in both the marketplace and on the mission field. "

My friend and business colleague Matt Sorger points out that Paul was both a tentmaker and an apostle. He wasn't working a nine-to-five job and trying to fit ministry in around it. He saw ministry and business as compatible. Matt believes God is releasing a "Joseph anointing" over His people. Just as God called Joseph and gave him the wisdom and creativity to establish a storehouse to save the people during a time of famine, so too God is blessing His people with a business anointing and strategies that will create storehouses of wealth.

"God has the ability to give us creative ideas, strategies, inventions, and business plans so we can *thrive* in both ministry and business to impact the world around us," Matt says. "God is a God of more than enough. He anoints our heads with oil and our cups run over. Jesus came to give us life more abundantly until it overflows. Knowing that this is God's nature gives us faith to receive all He has for us."

Matt was only recently introduced to health coaching. He had seen this health program work for other people and finally decided to give it a try after realizing his plans to lose weight and get in shape weren't happening on his own. Within a week, his body had changed enough for family members to notice and ask how to get in on it, and from there he got into the business side of it and began to flourish. Pastors and other ministry friends who had struggled with pain, inflammation, diabetes, exhaustion, and much more began experiencing transformation and renewed energy on this program. Matt knew then that God was calling him into this health business to help transform people not only spiritually, as he had long been doing, but also physically. Years ago, he had planned to become a doctor as a health-care provider. Now he's fulfilling that desire as an extension of his ministry as a health coach.

Again, this work of ministry and business is never either/or, as we've long been taught. It's both/and. Even though Matt has long had a very effective ministry, he believes ministry is bigger than what we have often believed. He says, "God wants to prosper people in business—to bring provision for them as well as make them so blessed that they are a conduit of Kingdom finances that can help change the world."

——— RECONSIDERING JESUS ———

One of the biggest obstacles to this paradigm shift is a misunderstanding of what we read in the Gospels. Many of us have gotten the impression that Jesus was always poor, with nowhere to lay His head. It seems to fit with the story of His birth, doesn't it? But if you're a woman, you can probably picture Mary's situation and relate to it. She's about to give birth. The pressure of her precious baby ready to come out coupled with jostling on the firm back of a donkey is about all she can handle. Any woman in her condition would be saying, "Get me off this ass *now*! I don't care where this baby is born, whether a field, the middle of the street, a cave, or a stable. Just find me a place to get this thing out of me!" Of course, with all due respect to the Messiah as the one bringing all the pressure.

Joseph was a businessman. If Joseph and Mary needed money, he could just build a table or a bed. I believe they had money for a room at the inn; there were just no rooms available because the city was fully occupied. So Joseph scurried to find a place—any place—for Mary to give birth.

What did the three wise men later bring Jesus? Frankincense, gold, and myrrh—extremely expensive stuff. That's wealth! The wise men brought Jesus extravagant gifts. We aren't told what happened to them, but we do know they were given to His family. They weren't dirt-poor.

When Jesus was dying on the cross, a group of Roman soldiers gambled for His garments. Why would Roman soldiers be gambling for a Jew's garments if they were rags? He hadn't died yet, so they had no open tombs, thunder and lightning, or glorious displays of God's power to make them think His robe might be valuable. Somehow we got the impression that it was made of burlap or another rough, simple material, but it had to be quite nice for soldiers to want it.

We have gotten the wrong impression about Jesus and His relation to money. It serves an important purpose in His Kingdom. God wants to raise up His sons and daughters who no longer embrace a poverty mindset as a testimony of their spiritual maturity, who understand their function as both priests and kings, whose hearts and minds have been tested, and who are prepared to move forward into the unexpected blessings He has for them.

5

Our Calling as Priests and Kings

Wrestling matches with God always involve turning points in our lives. Every time we wrestle with God, He wins—just like He did with Jacob—and we end up with a limp. But each time we wrestle with God and win, we are also raised up to a new level—like Jacob. When I wrestled with God on the floor in Toronto for two and a half hours, I got up with a limp, but my limp indicated I was being transformed. I didn't just get a touch or zap from God. It was life-transforming.

There's a difference between a touch and a transformation. Too many people in the body of Christ are looking for a touch from Him, and He gives it to them. But a touch can go away quickly. When you're transformed, you're changed for life. For example, if I stick a paper clip into a wall outlet, I'll get touched. I'll feel the shock, and the ends of my fingers might get charred. But if I climb up a utility pole and wrap my arms around the transformer at the top of that pole, I would be transformed! I would not be the same anymore. I wouldn't walk the same, talk the same, think the same, or live the same.

Most of the church is looking for a touch when God really wants to transform us, and that's what literally happened to me on that floor in 2003. I got up with a limp and did not walk, talk, live, or think the same way anymore. So I'm always after a transformation, not just a touch.

I had another wrestling experience with God about this idea of functioning as a king rather than just as a priest. I wasn't opposed to it; I loved the implications of it in terms of Kingdom impact. But I had a lot going on. How would I balance business and ministry? It was foreign enough to me that I had to tell God I wasn't sure how to do it all. I didn't know how to transition into it. We would need a business coach, a business attorney, and a financial advisor. How could I make all that work in light of everything else I was doing?

Unlike my baptism of love, this was not a matter of shifting my heart. I already had a heart for reaching kings and communities. I wasn't opposed at all to what God was doing. But I couldn't wrap my mind around it. I needed a mental transformation.

ENTERING THE WORLD OF KINGS

"We don't know how to be millionaires," we told the business coach in Utah we had just onboarded. We told him how our business had kept growing and how we had gotten to a point of realizing we needed help—and not from the sources we'd always relied on.

So many things in our lives were changing, and we knew we weren't prepared to navigate all the changes on our own. In the priest-king roles we found ourselves in, we wanted to know more about the king side of things—the world of the marketplace.

That's a common problem with believers in general, not just with us. We understand the priestly role—ministry, prayer, worship, evangelism, fasting, having a quiet time, and all the things we think of as spiritual—but we don't really know how to function in a kingly role or among people with that kind of calling or anointing. We don't always know how to manage people, finances, governments, and businesses.

So we gathered a team around us—our business coach, a financial advisor, and then a business attorney—and also got a ton of counseling from Leif. We listened to people in business and learned whatever we could—and still do. We've read just about all the books by Robert Kiyosaki and his team, beginning with *Rich Dad Poor Dad*, as well as many other people with expertise in this area, like Gary Keesee's books *Fixing the Money Thing*, *Money Mysteries from the Master*, and more. This whole body of expertise was like a revelation to us.

We told our son about *Rich Dad Poor Dad*, and he said, "Mom, I have that. It's packed away." A day or two later he dug it out and lent it to us, even though I had already ordered my own copy.

"This is amazing," I said. "Why didn't I ever know about this stuff?" I took a photo of the cover and texted it to Leif and said, "Have you ever read this book?"

"Yes," he said. "All my kids had to read it."

"Excuse me?" I laughed. "You had me read book after book about living out the priestly calling, but you never gave me this book?" I was hooked. Leif knew there were a lot of other areas I needed to work on before I could begin to read books about Kingdom wealth and abundance. Now we read every book we can get our hands on with this kind of teaching.

Kiyosaki's approach is based on growing a cash flow from four quadrants: E is for being an Employee. S is for being Self-employed, in which you may still have a brick-and-mortar building to go to and some financing to fund it, but you don't have any time because you have to run the business—although it usually ends up running you. B is for being a Business owner, which is a step further but still very time-consuming. And I is for Investor. In the course of five years, we had gone through every quadrant and were now in a position to invest—the I quadrant.

We had our business coach and financial advisors in place, and we wanted to invest in a property that could serve as a home away from home. We came close to buying a property in Orange Beach, Alabama, but three days from closing, that fell through. We looked at Punta Cana in the Dominican Republic, but during the height of Covid we wondered if we would always be able to get there when we wanted. (We ended up buying a place there more recently.) Then we looked at Sarasota,

Florida. We previously had two coaching events there and liked that area of Florida. Maybe that would be the spot.

As it turned out, there were a lot of reasons for us to move to Florida, not just to buy a vacation home there. For one thing, Florida is one of the few states without a state income tax. That was very appealing. But we also started thinking about business taxes. Tennessee's was 6.5 percent, which cost us $15,000 our last year there for just part of the year, and Alabama's was the same. But in Florida, it's 5.5 percent, and if you have an LLC, you're tax-exempt. That was a game changer for Ray and me.

We didn't want to leave our son and his family in Tennessee, but we also saw a lot of advantages to being in Florida—the beaches, the lack of taxes, and being much closer to Cuba, among others. So we said to our son, "We can give the money to the government, or we can leave it for you. We can stay in Tennessee and keep living around the corner from you or give you and your sister a greater inheritance."

It wasn't that difficult a choice for any of us, so we moved. And it wasn't too long before we got back to our original plan and invested in a property that could be our home away from home. BTW: our son and his family visit us often in Florida and they love it.

──── AN UNEXPECTED TURN ────

For people who have never had a retirement plan, being able to invest was a great position to be in. It was also vital for managing unexpected expenses.

In 2019, our term life insurance was expiring. We had gotten the policy as missionaries some forty years earlier, and it came to term. Of course, they wanted us to pay around $700 per month to retain it. The rates go up drastically with the passage of time, greater age, more health issues, and increased cost of living. Insurance policies don't cost what they did in our twenties.

We wish we had understood more about life insurance in our early years. We would have done things much differently. But back then, and likely today, most missionaries, pastors, evangelists, and ministers in general knew little to nothing about life insurance, investing, or managing any sort of wealth. I so wish we'd had someone like Leif in our lives many years ago to give us wise, godly counsel. That's one of the reasons for this book.

We figured we could do something else with the amount the insurance company was now expecting us to pay to keep our plan—like investing in rental property. We had learned a lot about stewarding our finances for the Kingdom and investing it in our family members' future and in the nations. As we saw our income increasing, we still wanted insurance. So our financial advisor found a plan that was so much better than a term policy. A time was set up for the nurse to come to our house and do all the testing—blood work, urine test, blood pressure, and the whole routine.

I passed with flying colors. Ray didn't. "Your heart is kind of skipping," she said. "You'll have to go in for a physical."

It took a couple of months for us to get him in for a stress test due to the Covid pandemic. He went in on a Thursday while I had a scheduled video call with a coach. In the middle of my call, I got a call from Ray. That was strange—he knew I had an appointment. I didn't answer.

Ray immediately sent me a text asking me to call him right away, which of course I did. He told me he had to go to the hospital and couldn't drive himself. The doctor wouldn't let him. Either I needed to go get him and take him to the hospital or he would have to go in an ambulance.

I contacted Sonia, our son, and our daughter as I drove out of the community where we lived. The rest of the day was a blur. I picked Ray up and drove him immediately to the hospital. When we got there, I wasn't allowed to go in because Covid was just getting started. Without any information to go on, I was wondering if he was going to have to have heart surgery or some other crisis intervention. I was completely in the dark, but they just told me to go home and wait for someone to call.

“ I picked Ray up and drove him immediately to the hospital. ”

After a few hours, I received word that I could go pick him up. They ran some tests at the hospital, and he left with three prescriptions, one that came with a coupon. When we went to get them filled at the pharmacy, they told us it was good that we had that coupon. Otherwise, that prescription would have cost $500.

That didn't really affect us because of how far we had come financially. But it left us wondering what people are supposed to do with something like that if they don't have insurance or that much out-of-pocket money, which is how we paid for it. It was a huge awakening to the financial stresses of American health care—something we had generally been able to avoid to that point in our lives.

We had a Zoom call with Ray's cardiologist the following Monday. The cardiologist told us he had a heart rate of 170 when he went in for the physical, which is on the verge of a stroke. That's why he wasn't allowed to drive himself to the hospital. The cardiologist also told us that Ray would have to have a cardiac ablation to prevent irregular electrical signals. That would help his heart rate get back to normal and stay there.

But the ablation got postponed several times, first when the doctor had an emergency and had to postpone it, then because Ray had Covid and wound up in the emergency room for that, and then because we went out of the country and were told upon return that he would have to wait. Finally, they were able to do the ablation on December 30, 2020, and it was a success. Thank you, Jesus!

Still, that question of how people manage these kinds of crises and those kinds of expenses if they aren't in the position we were in is a big one. I'm convinced God wants to bless His people, but not many are positioning themselves for that kind of blessing. If Leif had not been fathering us, training us, and speaking into our lives all those years, I don't know how we would have handled it. I wouldn't have been ready.

We must change the way we think about our relationships, our finances, and our health. The problem usually isn't primarily with our bank account, or our heart, stomach, or lungs. The deeper issue is what's going on in our minds.

I recently saw a video of a four-hundred-pound guy working out. He had had gastric sleeve surgery, which has become fairly common. I know several people who have done that, even a couple of times, but because their minds weren't in a healthy state, they gained most or all the weight back, and sometimes more. Eighty-three percent of Americans are overweight or obese. This is a health epidemic we must address, and our health program is doing just that.

We've prayed for many people over the years and seen God miraculously heal them. But if they just go back to the same habits that made them unhealthy to begin with, their healing might not last very long. Matt Sorger has experienced the same thing. "I can pray for them at the altar," he says, "but if they don't change the way they eat, if they aren't changing their nutrition, their health problems are just going to persist." The issue is not in our stomachs; it's in our minds.

It's the same with finances. Sometimes people come into a lot of money, whether through an upturn in business, an inheritance, or even the lottery. But if their mindset about money and their spending habits don't change, they often find themselves in debt or bankruptcy and once again trying to make ends meet. They get rich and then poor again.

But there's a difference between getting rich and acquiring wealth. Believe it or not, most people who win the lottery file bankruptcy within three years. Statistics show that 70 percent of lottery winners end up broke, and a third go on to declare bankruptcy.[1] Runaway spending, toxic investments, and poor accounting can burn through a lucrative windfall in next to no time—from (relative) rags to riches, then back to rags again. We'll see more breakthrough, healing, and wholeness when we minister to spirit, soul, body, and finances to holistically transform lifestyles as well as lives.

Acquiring wealth and learning how to steward it is a principle of the Kingdom of God. We must let God shift our perspective on the principle of Kingdom wealth before He can bless us the way He desires to.

Much of our work over the last few years has therefore involved educating ourselves about finances and wealth and then onboarding people into our coaching business and helping them understand finances and wealth as well. We believe this is key to what God is doing in our time, massively blessing His sons and daughters so we can fulfill the Great Commission. He wants to bless His people, but He also wants us to have the wisdom and mindset to be able to handle the blessing—and to multiply it in the lives of others. He wants us to build Kingdom wealth for carrying out His purposes. It's an invitation that His people need to prepare for and receive.

He loves how we pursue priestly things. Now He is raising up many to navigate the spheres of influence and societies of kings too.

---

[1] Statistics from the National Endowment for Financial Education.

—— THE KEYS OF THE KINGDOM ——

Before Cuba opened up, our spiritual sons and daughters in Cuba, the leaders of our ministry, were not allowed into tourist hotels. They couldn't even go in the front door. If we wanted to have a meal with them, it couldn't have been at the hotel restaurant. They would have had to wait for us outside.

After the passing of Fidel, Raul Castro changed the law so Cubans were allowed both to visit tourist hotels and to stay in them. I was back in Havana and brought my spiritual son Josué to stay with our team at the hotel. It was his first experience at a tourist hotel, even though he had lived in Cuba all his life. When I took him to the desk to check in, he was very nervous. He wasn't quite sure it was okay for him to be in there. I handed him his room key—a plastic card—and we headed to the elevator. I suggested we meet in the restaurant for dinner at 5.

He got off on his floor, and I pointed to his room before the elevator took me up to my floor. About five minutes later I heard a knock on my door. It was Josué.

"Mom, I don't know how to use this," he said. Mind you, Josué is a very sharp guy.

"Come with me," I replied. "I'll show you how to use the key, son."

So I went down to his room with him. "See this metallic strip? You just slide it through this slot and, *wham*, the little light turns green, the door unlocks, and you can open it."

83

Josué was amazed. But I only had to show him once. Once he was in that hotel room, he stayed there almost the whole time. He wanted to enjoy the air conditioning, the shower, and the TV. The key gave him access to everything he wanted in that room.

Everyone has a junk drawer for things they don't know what to do with. Pens, trinkets, keys, whatever doesn't go somewhere else ends up in that drawer. We have keys in our junk drawers that probably fit doors from several houses ago or padlocks no one remembers. I'll ask Ray, "Sweetie, do you know what this key goes to?" And most of the time he responds, "I have no idea." Keys become useless if we don't know what they belong to or where to use them.

Many in the church seem to have the same challenge. They know there are keys to the Kingdom, and they know the keys are not meant just to hang on the wall or sit in a drawer. Those keys unlock authority to loose and to bind and to access the resources of heaven. But they don't know what doors to put them in or how to use them. And by the way, this is plural. Jesus said, "I will give you the *keys* of the Kingdom." We have access to many Kingdom keys, not just one.

If we're going to step into our calling as priests and kings, we will have to learn what the keys of the Kingdom are for and how to use them.

I recently preached this in a conference in Cuba to about 175 women and took keys to give to all of them to emphasize the point that we need to know how to utilize the keys we've been given. And we need to know that not just any key fits into any door. There are different keys that are created for different purposes. Two of the most important are the key of honor and the key of favor. I've learned from experience that if we know how to use both of those keys, then many opportunities and blessings will open up for us.

The key of honor unlocks the door of favor. When you demonstrate honor, whether to a government leader, a mentor or teacher, or anyone else, you unlock the door to their heart. That's not why you do it; you honor people for the sake of honor. It's part of the character of God's Kingdom. When you do that from a pure heart, acceleration takes place in your life and in everything you touch.

Honoring Leif as my spiritual father has opened up many opportunities for me and connected me with many people I could serve and who were important to my destiny and assignment for the Kingdom of God. Again, I didn't honor so I could get something from Leif or anyone else. I did it because that's what Kingdom-minded folks do—not to get something, but to give. Giving honor and creating a culture of honor in your life will open the door of favor. Since becoming Kingdom-minded, not just salvation-minded, I've witnessed this more times than I can count.

> " Giving honor and creating a culture of honor in your
> life will open the door of favor. "

Favor is a key too. It unlocks the door to our destiny. This is what my second book, *A Journey to Your Identity*, is about. As we've seen several times, the honor given by Joseph, Daniel, and Esther to the rulers in their lives gave them favor and led to culture-shifting, Kingdom-transforming situations, and events. Joseph became the vice-ruler of a nation. Daniel turned the heart of the king and secured promotions for himself and his friends and protection for his people. Esther exposed a plot against her people and prompted the king to turn it around completely in favor of the Jews. They all knew how to honor without a hook, and as a result, they won the hearts of nations and culture leaders, and obtained favor. The key of favor unlocked their destiny.

There are many keys of the Kingdom, not just two, but these are the ones I have seen open many doors in my life again and again. In Cuba, I have gained tremendous favor with governmental leaders. As I've honored Leif, who's known as the "ambassador of love" in Pakistan, I have gained much honor in that nation.

We can win the hearts of kings, rulers, and pharaohs without compromise. Esther, Joseph, and Daniel did, and they transformed some of the most wicked, hardcore nations on the planet.

I've learned a lot about the keys of the Kingdom not only from Leif but also from Pat and Karen Schatzline, founders of Remnant Ministries and friends and colleagues of mine. Their story speaks powerfully into this calling as both kings and priests, and I'll let Pat tell it in his own words:

For many years, we traveled more than three million miles to many nations as leaders of Remnant Ministries, and we saw over two million people come to Christ. But over the years we began to feel stirred in our hearts. Something had to shift inside of us. We got tired of an honorarium on Sunday determining our dream on Monday.

While we were on the beach in 2015, as we were getting ready to do twenty-seven conferences in the coming months, God said, "I'm going to change you. I'm going to give you the keys of the Kingdom." I thought of Matthew 16:19, where Jesus promises the keys of the Kingdom to His followers, and Isaiah 22:22, where God promises the key of David to His servant, but I didn't know exactly what He meant.

He said, "Son, I want to release something new inside of you. I'm going to give you the anointing of the priest and of the king." We're told in 1 Peter 2:9 that we are a royal priesthood, or, in the original translation, a kingdom of priests. He began to stir that in my heart and said, "You're going to get my anointed healthy and wealthy. But let's start with you first."

God told me to take back my health. I found a health plan and lost seventy-two pounds, and Karen lost twenty-four pounds. But not long into it, we decided we needed to pay it forward.

Something shifted in us. We began to realize we could rescue people and stretch the timeline on their tombstone.

But something else also changed inside of us. We began to realize that we had a CEO anointing to raise up and transform lives not only in the church world but also in the public square. We began to realize that we could awaken people to dream.

One thing God spoke to our hearts was that He didn't ask us to die for the church. He already did that. He said He wanted us to go release the anointing and minister to people to awaken both the priest and the king in them and walk side by side with them. David is identified as both a prophet and a king (see Acts 2:30), and God began to stir in our hearts that it's time for people to step into their destiny as both. He showed us that it's okay to be both priests and kings.

That's not what we were taught growing up. It had to be one or the other, and if you're not careful, that can lead to an orphan spirit and a poverty mindset. But God showed me that it's okay to walk in the blessing. He takes joy in our prosperity. He gives the ability to create wealth, and He began to stir in me what we could do for the Kingdom when we break that poverty mindset and orphan spirit.

We're children of the King, and the Kingdom is so much bigger than we think. He began to show me that there's a moment when you shift your destiny and begin to pass on generational blessings to your children. God promises to bless those who walk in righteousness, and it's okay to live our dreams and walk in peace. God spoke to Karen one day and said her busyness was not a spiritual gift. We had to realize that it's okay to rest and have fun again.

You have no idea what God has in store for you. When you begin to step into that priest and king anointing, that entrepreneurial anointing, and you begin to realize that He can use you, He's going to give you ideas, dreams, and visions.

I've learned that frustration and agitation are the mother of intercession. If God is frustrating you, it's because He is stirring you to get up and do something different. There's a moment when you realize that you want to get to heaven with nothing left to do. When we step into that priest and king anointing, miracles begin to happen. We begin to live like we have never lived before.

The Bible says that hope deferred makes the heart sick, but a longing fulfilled is a tree of life (see Proverbs 13:12). When you remove the lid that you put on yourself and learn what the Father has for you, He will begin to release and launch you into fulfillment of the things He has put in your heart.

Since we made that decision, our whole family has been released into a different anointing. We've been launched into real estate, politics, and CEO anointings in the marketplace. Our story shifted when we began to realize that God will give His people the keys of the Kingdom to launch their destiny.

—— RE-PRESENTING GOD ——

The core of our calling as priests is to represent God to all humanity. That's what priests do. They also stand before God to represent human beings and bring their needs to Him. It's a mediating, interceding position that goes both ways.

This has huge implications for our calling as kings too. On my way to Sri Lanka a few years ago, I knew our schedule would be packed as soon as we hit the ground, so I was focused on sitting in business class during our last leg of the trip and getting some sleep over the remaining four hours. As soon as I got on the plane, I sat next to the window in my row. As it turns out, I wasn't going to get any sleep. A man soon came in and sat down next to me and started up a conversation.

"What do you do?" he asked.

I learned a long time ago not to start off telling people I'm a pastor because I know how that can kill a conversation.

I didn't even want to tell him I was a Christian because of the reaction that gets sometimes—like putting in their earbuds and tuning out. So I tried a different approach.

"I work for my Dad," I told him.

"You do?"

"Yes, it's amazing. I love working for Him. He's the best Dad in the world. So incredible." And I just kept bragging on God as my Dad.

Over the next three and a half hours, I found out my conversation partner was a banker from Holland doing business in Sri Lanka. By the end of the trip, he told me, "I've never heard anyone talk about God like you do." He thought doing good while he was on earth would be enough. I definitely left him with a lot to think about after that flight, and I knew God would send the next Kingdom-minded son or daughter to pick up where I left off.

I wonder how often we really represent God—or better, re-present Him—as an amazingly good Father who really desires to bless us. We wouldn't withhold blessings from our own children, and we don't want to give them heavier loads than they can handle. So if God is an amazingly good Father, with far greater desires than even our best intentions for our kids, doesn't that mean He wants to give to us out of His abundance and protect us from overwhelming need?

Of course it does. And that's what we need to be demonstrating for people. We need to be presenting Him as the extravagantly generous Father that He is.

I don't talk to people about God making them rich. But I do talk to them about gaining wealth and using it to expand God's Kingdom and bless their family and anyone else He wants them to bless. This banker from Holland was blown away by that concept because he had never heard a Christian talk about God as the giver of life-transforming, Kingdom-expanding wealth before—a sad fact, but nonetheless true.

I do the same when I'm getting my nails done or talking with a neighbor. I start bragging on God, my Dad, and by the end of the conversation they are asking me to pray for them. It opens up a doorway into their heart, so it's easy to pray and release the Kingdom over their lives. It's a much more holistic and encouraging picture of who God is, and it draws people into a relationship with Him better than most preaching does.

I've known people who grew up in the church and maybe even were involved in ministry come to discover that God is not who they thought He is. He was presented to them one way early in their life, and it took an entirely different demonstration of His goodness to discover who He really is. A pastor's kid who came to us in Teen Challenge told me after a few weeks, "I never knew this God you're teaching me about!" A lot of Christians could say the same thing.

That's the power of re-presenting Him as He really is— good, delighted with His children, and overflowing with generosity.

—— A ROYAL PRIESTHOOD TOGETHER ——

Our dual calling as priests and kings also requires connection. It is not a solo adventure. We need strategic partners.

Teamwork is essential in any Kingdom work. That begins with family and community—partners linking arms to accomplish more together than as separate individuals. In our business, we look for coaches who are relational, teachable, and hungry because that's the kind of people we need to fulfill the mission. We know that's not everybody's makeup, but it's what will help us fulfill our assignment.

The same is true in any Kingdom work. It is vital to link up with those who can help you leverage your gifts (and for whom you can help leverage theirs) for maximum impact.

> " Teamwork is essential in any Kingdom work. "

The last time I was in Cuba, I knew I would be preaching in churches. That's part of the mission. But my primary goal was to meet with people who are positioned to be culture-shifters on the mountains of society. It's fine to expand the Kingdom of God by addition. It's even better to expand it through multiplication. And you need strategic partners to be able to do that.

In fact, that has been a big shift in my assignment in Cuba in recent years. I still preach in churches and help with new church plants, partly because it's important but also out of the relationships I've built there. People get saved, and it's always glorious. Seeing someone get saved and go home living differently with their family is wonderful, and that can multiply, though it's usually a slow multiplication.

But if I can get two hundred Kingdom leaders from across the island in a room and help mobilize, equip, and empower them, and then they go out and multiply from their positions of leadership, that's leverage. When people are not just stepping into the Kingdom and figuring it out but are already Kingdom minded, that launches a powerful multiplication process. I'm all about getting people to heaven, but my assignment also includes getting heaven into people!

That's what Leif does in Pakistan and all over the world. He talks to groups of pastors and ministry leaders, a strategically important thing to do. That will always be part of his assignment. But when he speaks to the powerful and well-positioned leaders in mosques and wins their hearts, he suddenly becomes a Joseph speaking to thousands of pharaohs. That's ramped-up multiplication.

We have two responsibilities as Kingdom advancers. One is touching the beggars on the street corners and ministering to the people in the pews, and the other is going after the hearts of kings. The majority of priests know how to do the first and have been working on that front for ages. Few know how to do the second, which explains why we are not shifting cultures, environments, businesses, and nations very quickly. We've just been hanging out with other priests. But what if we had conferences with kings? That drastically expands our influence and our reach.

These are the vital components of a priest-king calling. This is how a holy nation and royal priesthood functions. We enter a new and greater realm of influence in...

- learning how to be ministers of wealth and stewards of heaven's resources;
- growing in our understanding of the keys of the Kingdom and learning how to use them as God intends them to be used;
- representing God truthfully and beautifully as priests at home in the world of kings;
- and leveraging strategic partnerships to advance God's Kingdom.

It's different from what we've always done, and that's a good thing. It promises to bring different and greater harvests of multiplied fruitfulness and blessing.

6

Culture-Changing Businesstry

When we talk about Kingdom wealth, it's important to understand that this is not a matter of building wealth simply in order to be rich or to build your own "kingdom." Many people think that when we teach abundance, we're actually encouraging excess, wastefulness, and personal extravagance on things that don't really matter. The implication is that anyone seeking abundance is essentially pursuing selfishness.

Kingdom wealth and the abundance God gives His children are different. He does want to bless us, and He does want us to enjoy the blessings He gives. He doesn't want us to place our trust in riches, but He "gives us richly all things to enjoy" (1 Timothy 6:17). But our understanding of wealth and abundance is not just about enjoying life more. It's Kingdom oriented. I don't want to have money for money's sake. I want to be able to fund ministry, advance the gospel, build the Kingdom in communities, and grow an inheritance to pass on to the next generation. Those are all Kingdom principles. The whole point is to be a channel of God's blessings to the world around us for His glory. The more He can trust us with His resources, the more of them He gives us.

Many people misunderstand the concept of financial freedom. Financial freedom isn't just about having an abundance of wealth. You can be free financially and not have an abundance of wealth. It isn't about the amount.

How does someone know they have financial freedom? How do they know they have money and money doesn't have them? How do they know they're free from money? When they can give freely and not begrudgingly. When they can be obedient to whatever God tells them to give and not have to question Him.

The more God can give through you, the more He will give to you. That's ultimately financial freedom.

This whole journey has stretched us in so many ways, and in very good ways, and it has been eye-opening. We've realized we and the people we've linked arms with are on a mission to get the word out to believers, and especially pastors and ministers. Many don't know or believe they can be pastors and prophets and prosper, executive pastors and entrepreneurs, missionaries, and millionaires at the same time.

The concept of "missionary and millionaire" is foreign to most people in the body of Christ. We have historically had a very narrow, limited mindset. And if the shepherds think that way, what else can we expect the flock to think?

While I was pastoring in Ohio but before we got involved in our health-coaching business, I spoke at a women's event at another church. The pastor confided in me, "I've got a couple of millionaires coming to my church. What should I do with them?"

This is not an unusual problem. When church people get close to millionaires, the temptation is to love them with an agenda of being financially blessed by them. It's a natural instinct, but it isn't Kingdom honor. We need to get comfortable with living among priests *and* kings.

When I first went to Ohio as a pastor, one of the first things I did was to look up the wealthiest man in the city. I had a seven-mountain mindset—that people in places of influence on the seven mountains of society are critical to the direction society goes.[1] The wealthiest man in the city happened to be an incredible man of God. He had long demonstrated a heart for upgrading the city with his financial investments and contributions.

> " When I first went to Ohio as a pastor, one of the first things I did was to look up the wealthiest man in the city. "

I made an appointment to go see him, and Sonia went with me since Ray was at work. The table in his boardroom was extremely long, and the many chairs around it looked like they had each cost a thousand dollars. I sat there with

---

[1] The seven mountains of society are government, economy (or business), education, arts and entertainment, media, family, and religion. If we carry Kingdom influence on all the mountains, not just the two mountains priests have historically focused on, and understand our role in shifting culture, society grows more Kingdom-like and more open to what God is doing in the world. This is a huge aspect of our calling.

him and introduced myself as the new pastor of Family of Faith Community Church, and we talked for a while. Then he asked, "What can I do for you?"

This was in those early days when our most desperate need was a new parking lot. It would have been very easy to ask him to fund it or at least contribute to it. We also had other needs that he surely could have helped us with.

"I don't really need anything," I told him. "I just wanted to come meet you. You're an amazing man. I've heard great things about you." I had brought a couple of books to give him, including Johnny Enlow's *Seven Mountain Mandate*, so I offered those to him and didn't ask for a thing.

"Can I pray for you?" I asked.

"Absolutely."

So we prayed for him and left.

I had already passed my tests on finances, and I knew the importance of honor. Like Joseph, Daniel, and Esther, who honored the rulers they served, I wanted to love and honor this "king" of the city without an expectation of anything in return. Afterward, I'd connect with him at a city-wide prayer breakfast or other events, always remaining with a heart of honor.

Like my pastor friend who confessed to not knowing how to treat the millionaires in his midst, most people serving in a priestly capacity don't know what to do with kings. Our priority with people—any type of person—always needs to be to love them and win their hearts.

I've done the same thing in Cuba. We have 350 churches in our network, and our leadership asked me what I wanted to do on one of my recent trips.

"I want to meet with key leaders," I told them, "mountain and culture influencers." I'd been teaching there long enough for them to know what I meant.

So that's what we did. I met with a lot of different business and government leaders, some at really high levels. I also spent some time shifting the thinking of our congregations there. Years ago, Kim Clement gave a word about Cuba that foretold it opening up, then closing again tighter than ever, then opening up again. It was very specific about the sequence of how things would happen, and what he predicted was unfolding during that time exactly as he had said it would. I have been hanging on to that word for fifteen years.

I asked our church leaders if they had heard of Kim Clement—some had, and others hadn't—and told them in detail about what he had prophesied. I had to be careful how I said things there, but they knew what I was talking about when I described certain shifts in the nation's leadership.

"In Kim's word regarding a major shift, we've witnessed that. The nation has opened up and you've been able to have your own businesses and make money to support your families," I said. Pastors there often made only $15 a month. "Some of you were doing well and even buying homes, and then as Kim said, things would shut down again, tighter than ever." Two years earlier, Covid had shut everything down so that hardly anyone could carry on with their business.

"A lot of you have lost your business in the last two years. But Kim said there would be another shift, and after that Cuba would become a Christian nation. That's where we are right now. It's going to be different now. You won't just be restarting a business to make money. You'll be creating a 'businesstry'—a business that also functions as a ministry. It's called marketplace ministry."

There isn't a good word for that in Spanish, so I spelled it out a little more. "Your businesses will be Kingdom ventures. There will be people who walk through the doors of your business who would never walk through the doors of your church. Your place of ministry will be in that business."

THINKING LIKE A KING

That's what Ray and I have developed: a businesstry. Our church (business)—our coaches alone number more than 2,200, and that number is growing. We've impacted more than 45,000 lives. Many of our coaches are not Christians and come from a completely different background, but as we coach them and win their hearts, they learn of Kingdom ways, because that's how we conduct our business. Our goal isn't to evangelize our coaching community—that would be using the company for something it never intended—but it happens organically anyway. Some have become Christians, and those who already were believers have built Kingdom wealth through it and are experiencing the Kingdom in their health, finances, and relationships. It's a business and a ministry—a businesstry.

One of our mentoring coaches coined that word in a book he wrote.[2] We use it to describe a business that also functions as a ministry because it is not a business just to make money but also to advance the Kingdom through whatever it does.

If people come through the doors of a business and are impacted by encountering God's people demonstrating God's character and ways, that's a businesstry.

If a business builds kingdom wealth that can be leveraged to fund ministry and create a generational blessing, that's a businesstry.

If the motive behind a business is to bless a community and draw people into a relationship with God, that's a businesstry.

It can take any shape or form, but what defines it as a businesstry is not just the goal of making a profit. It's to leverage that profit strategically—as well as the character of the business itself—for Kingdom purposes.

> If the motive behind a business is to bless a community and draw people into a relationship with God, that's a businesstry.

Ray and I recently hosted a three-day businesstry retreat for the top seventy-five coaches in our organization. We didn't make it just about business but also about ministry. We brought in Leif as a featured speaker. At least 90 percent of the coaches

---

[2] Doug Wood, *Church Boy to Millionaire: How to Find Personal Freedom and Liberate Your Millionaire Mindset for Massive Impact* (Aradaya Publishing, 2019).

who attended were believers. The other 10 percent left with an impression of God they did not have prior to attending.

One even approached me on our last night at our farewell dinner and asked, "Do you baptize people?"

"Yes" I said. "Many over the years."

"Will you baptize me? I need to get my life right with God."

After the dinner, we headed over to a swimming pool where I baptized her and another coach who was ready to start her life all over with God. A crowd of coaches stood around and celebrated with them. Now that is fun business and ministry.

The Kingdom-minded businessman I mentioned earlier used his wealth to build bridges, beautiful buildings, and nice retirement homes to bless the city of Newark, Ohio. It began when he and his wife were driving into Newark from Columbus one day and she said, "Entering Newark isn't very... well, beautiful."

That thought caught him by surprise. He realized the city didn't reflect God's Kingdom. So instead of complaining and agitating to get political leaders to fix things, they began the shift themselves. They had the wealth to do that. They were kings who knew how to utilize the resources they had to demonstrate God's care for communities.

One of our favorite statements in our health-coaching community is "Money in the hands of good people will do great things." And we do!

Priests don't generally think that way, mainly because they don't have the funds. There are a lot of priests living paycheck to paycheck. Many ministers have opted out of Social Security and have less than $1,000 in their bank accounts. I know one pastor who was selling plasma a couple of times a week to make ends meet for him and his family. He still has scars on his arms like a drug addict. Now he also has a thriving health-coaching business, no longer lives paycheck to paycheck, and doesn't sell his plasma anymore. Kings have the funds to accomplish a lot!

But why can't we embody both of those identities? If Jesus is our example as God's Son, a healer, a teacher, an evangelist, and a pastor, why not also as a priest-king? Instead of spending all our time crying out to God to transform our city—not a bad prayer at all, of course—maybe we should consider whether God is telling us to transform it. Why don't we learn to shift our mindset and step into businesses that will do that? The opportunities are limitless. Every sector of society and its marketplaces needs a touch and a transformation from God.

I like how Leif puts it. For years he has said that the church is crying out, "Come, Jesus, come!" But Jesus is saying, "Go, church, go! I'll come when you go!" Maybe our prayer should not be for God to transform the culture but to raise up culture transformers—and realize that we are part of the answer to that prayer.

We see this happening all around the world. Paul Yadao and his family of believers in the Philippines are shifting cultures there because they started to live as kings and not just priests. The city of Redding, California, has been significantly impacted because the people at Bethel didn't just remain priests; they became kings. They bought the civic center and took on that responsibility because they didn't want the city to shut it down and lose the blessing it could bring. That's kingly thinking.

Mark Walker, a business owner on the West Coast, sensed God's call in his early 20s to become a generous giver into Kingdom work. He didn't have a business at the time, or even an idea for one or any money to start it, but he knew God had planted this calling in his heart. God gave him not only an idea but also the resources to begin his business, and over time, as he and his wife gave sacrificially into God's work wherever they felt led to do so, the business grew—from one furniture store into a couple more and eventually into an entire chain run on Kingdom principles. The business not only made money; it became a ministry to customers, employees, and the communities it operated in.

Within twenty years, this furniture business went from just an idea to a multi-million-dollar operation that, according to Mark, "went way beyond our abilities and skills." Now at more than forty years, it has annual sales of more than $60 dollars. Every step of the way, God revealed how faithful He is to fulfill His promises. Mark and his family have functioned as both priests and kings. They may not have put that language to it early on, but those are the roles they have stepped into, and they have had an enormous impact by running their business as a businesstry.

David Green has run his business that way too, and with a huge impact. He was one of six children in his family, and his father pastored small churches, so they never had a lot of money. When all of David's siblings went into some sort of ministry as pastors or wives of pastors, he thought he was the black sheep of the family for doing something else. But David started a business that carried the heart of a ministry, not only in meeting the needs of clients and customers but also in treating employees well. He decided from the start to build the business on biblical principles. He began with $600, and though the business nearly went under in the mid 1980s, it eventually recovered and thrived. Hobby Lobby now has more than 700 stores, 35,000 employees, and $4 billion in sales.

Hobby Lobby's identity as a businesstry was especially prominent in its case against the government that went all the way to the Supreme Court. The company faced potential fines of over a million dollars a day if it did not provide abortion-inducing prescriptions under the Affordable Care Act. That went against Green's values and those of the company culture he had established. They experienced numerous obstacles and setbacks, but they stood their ground. The Supreme Court's decision not only vindicated Hobby Lobby; it also established a precedent that allows businesses nationwide not to compromise their values while also treating employees well and with honor.

These principles and values are highly transferable. It's good to aim for functioning as kings, establishing business-tries, and growing Kingdom wealth in our own lives, but there's a greater opportunity too. It's time for God's people to train up others to think this way and live it out. When I pastored in Ohio, I would have other people on our staff preach even when I wasn't out of town. I'd sit on the front row and cheer them on. When I minister in Cuba, I want to instill Kingdom thinking and impart Kingdom ways to our pastors and leaders there rather than just coming in and leading for them. It doesn't do any good to train people to do things if we never allow them to actually do them. The entire body of Christ needs training in Kingdom thinking and living as both priests and kings on every mountain of society.

——— A MULTI-MOUNTAIN MINDSET ———

I told our church leaders in Cuba that they still needed to be praying for government leaders in the nation to come to Christ. That was an important part of their ministry. But what if God was opening doors to the mountain of government or the mountain of economy for them? What if they knew how to walk through that door without flipping out because they didn't agree with government leaders, but instead by carrying the Kingdom with them? Many of them didn't think they were ready for that. So I did some teaching around that calling:

Kings shift cultures; priests don't.

Kings hold the keys to unlock doors; priests don't. Keys belong to the Kingdom.

Priests go to kings for a handout, but kings go to priests for a blessing.

Priests intercede. Kings go to war.

Priests pray. Kings make decrees.

Kings don't hang out with priests. They hang out with other kings.

Kings, not priests, are at the top of mountains, societies, and spheres of influence.

Kings have jewels in their crowns (the mind). Priests have jewels on their chest (the heart). We're called to activate not just our hearts as priests but also our minds as kings. It's time for God's sons and daughters not just to feel the heart of Jesus for people, societies, and nations but to think with Kingdom wisdom like Jesus does and impact people's lives.

Through the prophet Samuel, God sent a king, Saul, to conquer the "hill of God" where the Philistines, the enemy, were (1 Samuel 10). He sent a king, not a priest. Kings are the ones who conquer mountains for God.

There's a reason Jesus told Paul he would proclaim His name to Jews, Gentiles, *and kings* (see Acts 9:15). This realm of influence is very important to God. I invest my time shifting people's mindsets because priests need to learn how to be kings and how to function in the marketplace. That's where society's change-makers live. Kids play "king of the mountain," not "priest of the mountain," because they easily understand the influence of position. That's where culture shifts come from. As kings, we shift the culture in societies and transform nations.

> " He sent a king, not a priest. Kings are the ones
> who conquer mountains for God. "

No one illustrates this better than my friend Michael Mauldin, a minister, film producer, and motivational speaker. Michael and his wife are the driving force behind the Upper Room worship and prayer movement and the film *Superspreader* about Sean Feucht and his worship events. As a king and priest, he has demonstrated what it looks like to influence the world with the excellence of kings.

> When we're kids, we have dreams of what we want to be when we grow up—football players, lawyers, doctors, princes and princesses, mothers, and fathers... we love to envision a beautiful future. My dream growing up—don't laugh—was to be in the mafia. I grew up in a broken home and didn't have any experience in church. I was "discipled" by people like Al Pacino, Martin Scorsese, N.W.A., and Snoop Dogg—filmmakers and rappers who gave me a vision of the world that looked like people who were willing to lay down their lives for each other. They at least had a code of honor. They would never rat on their friends. I eventually realized I was longing for unconditional love, and the only version I saw of it was in these films and media productions.

When I got saved, I realized what true unconditional love was. Jesus said there's no greater love than laying down your life for your friends (see John 15:13). God put this truth in my heart, but it was only realized through Christ. I'd seen a perverted version of it in films and music. So when I got saved, I had a strong desire to transform culture through arts and media because I knew we'd been entrusted with the greatest stories the world has ever known—the stories that hold the keys to life and human flourishing. I just hadn't seen the right role models telling these stories in a cool and relevant way so that the next generation could behold the beauty and nature and heart of Jesus.

That dream was put on hold, as I got married and ended up doing mission work in the Middle East. When I eventually came back to Dallas, my wife and I helped plant a church called The Upper Room, we built the foundations of Upper Room Worship, and I became an executive pastor for about seven years. We were seeing revival—multiple church plants, and young people coming to Christ in great numbers and being baptized, getting set free, delivered, and made whole. Yet I was still seeing the culture around us sloping downward.

We went through a very rough season in 2017. I had just gotten off the mission field in northern Iraq, and my brother committed suicide. Then I dealt with a youth minister dying of cancer, the death of my grandmother, and another friend's death from a heart attack a week later. I also wrestled with a betrayal during that season, so it was just a very difficult time.

I retreated to spend some time with the Lord and asked Him a question that I'd encourage everyone to ask Him: *What big thing do you want to accomplish through my life?* I already knew my identity—who I was in Christ—and I understood that life was about intimacy with Jesus, being one with Him. But Jesus also had a mission to seek and save that which was lost, to destroy the works of the devil, to reach the world beginning in Judea, then Samaria, then to the ends of the earth. So I asked Him, *What do you want to do through me?*

"I want people to see the heart of My Son," He said. And as I was writing this down, I wrote "SEE" in big letters. I also felt as if He wanted His stories to be told in the earth. And third, that He wants His sons and daughters to possess the gates of the enemy. This was one of the promises given to Abraham, the father of our faith, so if this is his promise, it's ours too.

When I thought about "the gates of the enemy," what came to mind was the entertainment media complex—that gateway that had influenced and discipled me as a kid. The dreams that

God had put in my heart at an early age were being reawakened. I felt called to step out in faith, away from "ministry" (as we traditionally understand it), and into telling God's stories, specifically through film. But I knew that to truly influence and impact our culture, I had to be able to tell God's stories in an excellent way. The films I created had to be on par with, or even greater than, those created by Hollywood, where the tone and tenor were set for what we've digested as a culture. So the first film I made was *Superspreader* about the Let Us Worship movement.

The Bible says that a man excellent in his craft will stand before (or with) kings (see Proverbs 22:29). So to be a king or to stand with kings, you have to be excellent in your craft. In whatever God has called you to do, it has to be at a level that is recognized at the top in the marketplace, government, education, etc. If we want to be influencers and shapers of culture in the world around us, we have to be so excellent in whatever we do that the world takes notice.

God has infused His creativity in all His children so that whatever we create will influence the world. I was recently with a businessman who told me about a maker of instruments. This man told me that he walked into the craftsman's shop and began to cry. The work was so beautiful and accomplished, and the sacrifice that went into it was overwhelming. And in God's economy, fire falls on sacrifice. So when this businessman saw the sacrifice of this man and the quality of his work, he could not help but weep.

That's a profound example for all of us and for wherever you are at this point in life—that whatever God wants to accomplish through you, you would do it with excellence and be able to stand among kings, have influence, and shape our culture for His Kingdom, revealing His heart to a generation.

I truly believe the next great move of God will take place in the marketplace. Jesus didn't go to the priests to turn the world upside down 2,000 years ago. He went to the marketplace. He knew He could impact the world with the message of salvation and love with entrepreneurs. Please hear my heart here. I love the church. But if we could transform cities and nations entirely through the church, we would have already done it by now. But we haven't. God is raising up entrepreneurs again in our time—marketplace ministers who are impacting lives and transforming cultures to turn the world right-side up. Entrepreneurs know how to network. Most pastors don't. Most pastors' mindsets are, *You do your thing; we'll do ours. You worship your way; we'll worship ours.* Then we wonder why we're not transforming communities.

There was a time when Ray and I didn't know how to sit in a room of millionaires and be comfortable. We would have had no influence there because we didn't know how to function in that environment, with kings. Now we do. And God wants to raise up many more who know who they are and can function as both priests and kings.

I've served on the mountain of religion for most of my life, but I've also learned to put my feet on other mountains too. I stepped onto the government mountain as a law enforcement chaplain. I was actually issued a key to the main government building in our county the day after I had preached at our church on utilizing the keys to the Kingdom—I took it as a prophetic statement of receiving the key to the government mountain!—and now I'm firmly planted on the mountain of business too. We must have our feet on the mountains of kings and learn how to navigate them without falling off.

We have a lot of priests in our coaching organization who are still wondering, *Does God really want to bless me?* They still have a hard time seeing themselves making money. I haven't had that problem for many years now, but many Christians and ministers do.

That's because the church has long specialized in the mountains of religion and family. But God is equipping His people to walk through the doors of the mountains of government, economy, media, education, and entertainment, carrying the Kingdom with them. This is what changes nations and what I encouraged our leaders in Cuba to start activating. The time has come for it—and many other nations—to become a Christian nation, and the only way for that to happen is for God's people to show up on those mountains with an understanding of how to function there as priests *and* kings. When that happens, cultures will be transformed.

—— WINNING THE HEART BEFORE THE MIND ——

We've had to coach some of the coaches in our organization not to use "Christianese" in their business relationships. It's not that we want them to hide their faith—not at all. But the language we use in a business environment can be alienating to a lot of people, and that cuts off the opportunity to continue relating to them effectively. We want to keep the relationship open.

We have coaches who tend to work some preaching into their stories. We encourage stories—every leader who does some speaking or training is invited to share their story of how they first got into the business. My story is God speaking to me on the way to Pakistan about getting hold of my health so I could finish well, and how my response was, "I don't know what to do because I don't know of a diet that has worked for anyone." But I emphasize my realization that this was not a diet, not the part about God's speaking. That's just how it came to me.

But some of our coaches don't realize they are preaching to a very diverse group with a variety of religious backgrounds and different lifestyles, many of whom don't want anything to do with God. Preaching and speaking Christianese are not the keys to open the doors to people's hearts. With that approach, we're generally trying to open their minds and get people to think like we do. Jesus didn't go after people's minds. He went after their hearts, and as He won their hearts, He was able to change their thinking.

When we take a different approach and win people's hearts, they will listen to us. They don't have to, and we don't force that, but doors tend to open. If it's a Kingdom business, not just a means to make money, it eliminates some of those barriers. We find people walking into our business who would never walk into a church, and they're coming to Christ.

> " When we take a different approach and win people's
> hearts, they will listen to us. "

One example is a young couple who came into the program and together lost more than 270 pounds. They went through a phenomenal transformation in their health, including their weight. They became coaches. The coaches at levels between us and them are amazing, strong believers, but this couple said very clearly that they didn't want to hear anything about religion from any of us.

So we decided just to love on them. We didn't bring up "religion"—I never talk in those terms, but God equaled religion in their minds. We just loved them as human beings, with no agenda or expectations. Maybe we would win their hearts, or maybe they would continue to keep their distance from our faith. But we wanted to love and honor them regardless.

After about a year, they won an incentive trip with us to Cabo San Lucas. I felt God speaking to me to take them a copy of my first two books, *A Christian Life Without Father God* and *A Journey to Your Identity*, a thirty-day devotional. I also took them a book by Robert Kiyosaki. The first morning we were there, we sat with them to have breakfast, and about forty-five minutes into it, I picked up the gift bag with the books in it and gave it to them. They pulled out the Kiyosaki book first and thanked us. Then they saw the next two books and realized they were mine.

"Listen," I said, "if you don't want them, throw them in the garbage. I won't be offended."

"No, we'd never throw away anything you gave us," they said. We'd won their hearts.

We opened a conversation with them about their background. We wanted to hear their story, and it became clear that they never had a very good representation of God in their lives as a father figure. They kept talking negatively about religion.

"Do you like it when people call our program a diet?" I asked.

"No, of course not. It's not a diet." We always avoid that word because our program is better described as a transformational health program with a weight loss component. Some people go through it for reasons entirely different from losing weight.

"Well, God doesn't like religion any more than you like coaching a client who thinks it's a diet," I said. "He doesn't want to do religion with you. He wants a relationship with you."

It was like a light bulb went on for them, and we began to explain that God delighted in them as a son and daughter and created them to spend time with Him—that He loved them like a dad. "'Father' is His favorite name," I said.

We spent a couple of hours talking with them. The following Sunday we were about to go out on a sailboat excursion with some other coaches. We had breakfast with this couple again before the excursion, just talking with them some more, getting to know them, loving on them, and doing life together. Then we had to go to our rooms to put on our swimsuits so we could go on the boating excursion.

While we were at the shuttle bus waiting, we realized another couple that was supposed to be in our group hadn't shown up yet. They were pastors from California and coaches in our organization. Ray texted to find out what was going on with them and to let them know the bus was waiting.

"We'll be right there," they texted back. "We just led Lyndsey and Travis to the Lord in the swimming pool!" They had no idea what had been going on the last year and a half with this couple, but they were there at the right moment. They called over two other pastors to take over and left the pool for the excursion.

I got on a video call with Lyndsey after we got home from our trip and asked her what happened, and she told me how they had accepted Jesus. She wanted to know what they were supposed to do now. I asked if they had a Bible, and they didn't, so I told her I would send them one.

A couple of weeks later, we were on another call. She said the Bible was on their nightstand. "What do we do with it?"

"Open to the book of John and the book of Psalms"—I explained how to find them— "and read a chapter from each of those every day. But before you read, ask God to show you yourselves as His son and daughter and Himself as your Dad."

About two weeks into that, they had finished John and wanted to know what to do next. I sent them to Acts and told them to do the same thing. A couple of months later, they asked if we could help them find a church. They had probably never been to one other than for a wedding or funeral, yet they had walked through the open doors of our business, and from there eventually they found their way into a body of believers. It was a dramatic turnaround, and it happened through our businesstry because we focused on their hearts and the relationship before ever trying to talk to them about what we believed.

We have a lot of coaches in our group who are atheists, agnostics, or from another religion, often living lifestyles that don't reflect an openness to the Kingdom message. I'm sure many see God through the lenses of how they perceived their fathers and mothers, and it's not always a good impression. That's how I saw God for many years too. I thought He didn't have time for me. If I needed anything, I would go to my brother, Jesus, and let Him approach the Father for me. We work with many people who have a skewed or discolored view of God or don't see how He fits into their lives.

I love winning people's hearts and giving them Kingdom lenses so they can see as Jesus sees, with Kingdom eyes.
Christians often pray, "Jesus, give me your heart for my city,
for so-and-so," and so on, but we should also pray for Jesus'
eyes so we can see our cities and the people in our lives as
He does.

We do not make it a practice to talk God or Christian-
ity with most of our clients and coaches, though they know
our story. Most have gotten to know me through meetings,
conferences, and on Zoom calls, and some of them listen to
my podcast now. "We didn't know we were signing up for
church," they've said. And they weren't. But we've won their
hearts, and we now have their ear. They have welcomed us
into their lives, and our responsibility is to love on them.

Jesus said that people would know we are His because
we love (see John 13:35). What if every church in America,
better yet, the world, stopped everything they're doing and
took a four-week course on just loving people? I have a strong
feeling our churches, communities, cities, and nations would
look very different.

It works the other way too. For a year and a half when we
first got started with our business, I never used the platform
at our church to preach or promote our program. They saw
the evidence—I was melting away—but I never talked about
it from the platform until my last message there before we
transitioned to Nashville, when I preached on "The Power of
Decision." So just as I never used the pulpit to sell the business, I don't use the business to preach the gospel. I don't have

to. When you're living the Kingdom in front of people, they are drawn into it without you having to sell it.

Leif is great at this. When he goes to Pakistan, people call him the ambassador of love. He has always gone in with love first, and winning hearts has opened doors for him to speak to minds.

That's always what it comes back to: winning the heart before going for the mind—the Joseph, Daniel, Esther, and Nehemiah approach. They influenced minds, but not until they captured hearts. Only then could they shift the way their rulers thought. And only like that can we go in and transform cultures and complete the Great Commission.

7

The Rhythm and Responsibility of Businesstry

We met with Leif a couple of years after that conversation when he urged me to wipe the table clean and reset my priorities. I had resigned my chaplaincy and some of the women's events I was doing so I could focus more on my core areas of ministry and the "teacup saucer" of our health-coaching business that was growing on the side. I had learned what to say no to, either for a season or perhaps forever, in order to strengthen my yes in the areas God was highlighting and grow in the kingly anointing.

By this time, that teacup saucer had become a big platter serving thousands of people. God had given us extraordinary grace during the Covid years, and the business had grown by more than 200 percent. I was once again at a point where I needed some advice on how to handle the different demands.

"How do you balance ministry and business?" I asked.

"You don't," Leif told me. "You learn the rhythm."

That was a powerful concept. I'd never really thought of it before.

Most of the people in the Bible who carried God's Kingdom and changed the world, including Jesus, were not priests by profession. Some were, but most were from the marketplace. Abraham and the patriarchal family; Israel's greatest kings; prophets who came from a variety of professions and spoke God's message to priests and kings; even the apostle Paul, who had religious training but a profession of tent-making—they all knew the ways of the marketplace.

That tells us a lot. This is the shift that needs to happen within the church. Jesus went to a group of guys who fished, collected taxes, immersed themselves in politics, and more. Paul took Aquila and Priscilla, a couple who were in business, and used them greatly as priests and kings to expand the Kingdom of God. They all knew the power of money for good and for bad, and they understood the kingly side of leadership. They weren't priests who had to learn to rule; they were businesspeople who had to learn ministry. They watched Jesus do all His miracles and work a priestly understanding into their worldly minds.

Getting that rhythm between priest and king has been one of the hardest things for me to learn. I came from years of a priest-oriented background—ministry. Now I had been led powerfully into a kingly activity—business. I've long known how to preach, evangelize, pray, prophesy, and pastor. That's the heart of what we do. But the king is the mind. I've had to be very intentional, not about balancing them as two different things, but about understanding the rhythm between them as integrated components of my life.

It takes a lot of effort to try to balance these two aspects of our calling. If we transform cultures by being at the tops of the mountains, and we want to change the trend of priests hanging out mainly with priests while kings hang out with kings, we must find the rhythm. Balancing or juggling them would be like running up one mountain to have influence there, and then running down it and up the other one to have influence there. It's trying to have one foot on each and therefore not having significant influence on either. That's exhausting.

But a rhythm of leaning into one and then leaning into the other, and sometimes recognizing that we're in both at the same time, that's a different story. It takes much less effort to go with the flow or the rhythm of being present on each or both as the situation calls for it.

Balancing is like trying to juggle plates while standing on one foot. I'm not into acrobatics, so it was a relief for me to know I didn't need to balance ministry and business. But I've been a percussionist since I was 12, so I understand rhythm. I knew Leif well enough to know what he was trying to communicate. I needed to lean into heaven and learn God's rhythm regarding ministry and business. I had exhausted myself trying to have my priest life and my king life as separate callings. They weren't. So my perspective had to shift.

Ministry is so ingrained in me that it's supernaturally natural to me. What I've really had to focus on is allowing business to become supernaturally natural to me as well so I can intertwine the two together. Like a dance, I needed to flow with rhythm—in this case, a Kingdom rhythm—so I wouldn't trip all over myself. It has been a challenging lesson, but getting into a good rhythm in business and ministry creates a beautiful dance called businesstry.

THE MAKING OF A KING

You can only be a king or queen by being born into royalty. And we are—that's what being born again accomplishes for us. We become sons and daughters of the King. But Esther, one of my heroes, didn't become a queen overnight. First she was a daughter with a spiritual father, Mordecai—the cousin who raised her. She had to know she had him as a father and be secure in him. But this spiritual dad also studied the king. He was at the king's gate daily, observing the king's behavior. He knew how kings thought and operated.

I believe Esther asked him about what he had seen each day when he came home. As they sat down to eat by the light of a candle on their dinner table, Esther would say, "Tell me what the king did today. I heard they are having a big festival. What does he like to eat? What's his favorite sport? What's his favorite hobby?" She never knew she would one day be taken by force to the palace as a potential queen. But she had an advantage over all the other virgins who were taken because she had a spiritual father who came home every night and told her about the king.

I believe one reason God's sons and daughters do not know how to hang out with kings is that we lack true spiritual fathers and mothers today—people who study *the* King, as well as kings on the top of the seven mountains of society, who teach their sons and daughters about them.

Esther's identity as a daughter came first, long before her position as a queen. That's how it works; we must know we are sons and daughters of the King before we live as royalty. Many believers today are trying to rule and reign without being solid in their identity as a son or daughter, and it doesn't work.

I knew my identity as a daughter of the King—that was my massive transformation in my baptism of love in Toronto. But I was still learning how to function as a queen, and it didn't come naturally. It was easy going from ministry to business. I could be praying for someone at the end of a service about whatever was going on in their life and speaking prophetically over them, and if they followed that with a question, "What's this health thing you're doing?" I could easily shift into a conversation about it. I'd been doing ministry for years and transitioning into a conversation about something else after ministering happened all the time. But going the other way was another matter. If I was speaking at a coaching event and someone came up to me afterward to ask if I would pray for them, I'd stumble. The shift was awkward. It would take a few seconds to get into that mindset and say, "Yes, of course I can pray with you. I do that too."

We once had a weekend event in Gatlinburg for our coaches, and the night after a long day of talking business, a couple came up and said, "We need to talk to you."

I thought they had some business questions. That was the context of the whole day, so I was in that mode. But when we sat down to talk, they asked what it would take to be our spiritual son and daughter. They wanted us to father and mother them like Leif had fathered Ray and me. I felt like a deer caught in the headlights.

We already had plenty of spiritual sons and daughters, so that wasn't the issue. We knew how to do that. But not in that context. That's when Leif's advice about rhythm became very apparent to me. I had to learn the ebb and flow not of talking about business and shifting into a ministry mindset but of being simultaneously in both realms, because they are key elements of the Kingdom. The dynamics had changed. And as it turned out, we embraced that beautiful couple as a spiritual son and daughter.

Shannon Grove, a state senator in California, beautifully demonstrates the heart of both a priest and a king. She grew up in a family that didn't have much money, and even though her mother often took her to church, she didn't like it very much and often got into trouble as a teenager. When she joined the army, she felt like she was running away from God.

Shannon served in Frankfurt, Germany, and was there when the Berlin Wall came down in 1989. It was in Germany where she found the Lord waiting for her "with His arms open wide." She dedicated her life to Him, and when she returned to the U.S. after her term of service, she worked for a couple of staffing agencies before eventually starting her own. I'll let her share the rest of her story and her heart for carrying the Kingdom first into business and then into government:

> One of the most incredible things you can do for somebody beside leading them to the Lord is to provide them with a job. A job is the best solution to poverty. The business we started on a dirt road has now flourished to one of the largest independently owned staffing agencies in California. Every day, we get to give people a job to provide for their families. Every day, we get to tell them that God gave them this gift. We've guided and prayed over countless employees who were given second chances and opportunities to stay out of prison. We really take care of our employees. We tithe off of our business and fund a lot of nonprofits in our community. It's a beautiful gift, this businesstry the Lord gave me.
>
> I wasn't looking to get into politics. Politics came looking for me. My congressman called and asked if I'd consider running for the state assembly, and I politely told him no. But I prayed and fasted about it with a dear friend for twenty-one days—a Daniel fast—and felt I was called to the

position. So we put my name on the ballot. We won, and I ended up in the California state legislature.

Many people had prophesied over me—Cindy Jacobs, who said I would be a woman of many firsts, as well as Kris Vallotton, Stacey Campbell, Ché Ahn, and many others. It's hard to believe a single mom who didn't go to college would be where I am today. But God!

I built significant relationships in the California Senate. The Lord provided a way for me to reach people across the aisle, many of whom had very different opinions from mine as a conservative. He opened doors for me to pray with some of the most powerful people in the world and send recorded prophetic words to many in the government.

Bethel Church in Redding once brought a group of students from their school of ministry to speak prophetic words over people in the capitol building. They would get words for a "modest O" or an "Irish James," and I knew exactly who those names applied to. By the end of the afternoon, several legislators had come to the rules room to be prayed over. One student kept saying he had a word for a Daniel, and we couldn't find anyone by that name. We looked on the Internet to see if we'd missed anyone's middle name, but no one came up. But this student kept insisting we had to pray over this person because he had brain cancer.

I did know someone with brain cancer, but his name wasn't Daniel. "What does he do?" the student asked.

I told them he was the chief of staff to the speaker, the most powerful person in the assembly. The young man looked at me and said, "Oh, he's Daniel, the servant to the king."

We reached out to the speaker's office but couldn't make contact. So we recorded the word from this student about how God was going to heal his cancer and his family wouldn't be abandoned. It was a beautiful word, and we shared it with this man the next day.

We've brought other people in to prophesy over other legislators. Sean Feucht came and led a worship event at the state capitol in the midst of Covid, and 12,000 people came. The residue of that worship service has continued to saturate our building.

My first two years in the Senate, I thought I failed at everything. I failed at every piece of legislation I tried to pass and at every piece I tried to stop. I really struggled with that. But the Lord spoke to my heart and said, "I asked, 'Who shall I send?' and you answered, 'me,' with no conditions laid out." I learned very quickly and spent time on my knees, and I know I'm here because I'm willing and because God called me. He's using me to share His love with all the people in the capitol building, whether legislators or staff. That doesn't prevent me from speaking godly, anointed, courageous truth, but I've learned that it's not about the battle or the victory. It's about obedience and being exactly where God has called me to be.

> " He's using me to share His love with all the people in the capitol building, whether legislators or staff. "

I could share story after story of things that happen in that building that prove God is there. I once walked down several flights of steps complaining to God about being alone, and when I walked out, I saw a beautiful lady who walked toward me, looked at me, and told me I was never alone. I have an incredible staff and am surrounded with believers in my office who love the Lord. We are called for such a time as this and for the purpose the Lord has put in us. We know He has a plan and purpose for our lives, and every day we show up to see what He has in store for us.

You can see in Shannon's testimony someone who has learned the rhythm of being a king and a priest at the same time, ministering in the context of both business and government. Learning this rhythm is how we get to the tops of the mountains to shift cultures. We can't just do it as priests. Priests have little influence there. Jesus was both a King and a Priest, the perfect demonstration of how to blend the heart of a priest with the wisdom of a king.

The king of Persia did not marry a priestess, even though Esther had a priest's heart. He married a daughter of Mordecai and, more importantly, a daughter of God because Esther had been raised up to understand how kings think. Another Persian king did not send Nehemiah to rebuild Jerusalem's walls because he was a priest; he sent him because he was a good administrator who understood the king's purposes. Pharaoh did not make Joseph second-in-command in Egypt because Joseph had spiritual understanding but because Joseph had strategic wisdom and a plan to protect the kingdom's interests. This is why we need to rise up with both the heart of priests and the mind of kings and live in a rhythm that honors both.

We're connected with some government leaders in Cuba who tell us that God is opening up gates into the highest levels of government as well as on the mountains of education and business. It's already happening in many places. Assignments at the University of Havana have included reading the Old Testament and researching the church—in a country that has been hostile to religion and faith for over six decades. There is opportunity to lead many of the top leaders there to salvation in Christ and help transform the culture—something every believer there would want. But are they ready to enter in? Are we ready to enter into the spheres of influence God is opening up to us in our own country?

Some are, however, it's a matter of understanding both the priestly and kingly roles and learning to operate in both. I've had to train myself not to think in terms of stepping into the kingly in my business and stepping into the priestly in my ministry. These two realms are not separate. The old sacred-secular divide we've adhered to for so long is not a Kingdom way of life.

——— THE WAY OF STEWARDSHIP ———

In order to walk in your destiny as a priest and king, you'll need to steward it well. Every step of the way, God gives you responsibilities, tests, relationships, resources, gifts, and assignments, and how you respond to them will either set you up for advancement or send you back through those steps again. You'll find that your success very often depends on your ability to keep your focus on the right things and not get distracted with false whys or impure motives.

When Cuba loosened many of its policies and our leaders there could open up a personal business, they were quick to get started. Many had been making $15 a month and suddenly had an opportunity to make five or six times that. They started opening hair and nail salons, restaurants, or whatever they were good at or interested in. But within a few short years of launching their businesses, Covid shut them down. Most of them lost the businesses they had started.

Now that things are opening up again, the mindset needs to shift. They need to steward their new opportunities with a different perspective. They need to see their work as a Kingdom business that not only makes money but also brings people through the doors they would otherwise never reach. They will make money, but they can't make money the focus. The why, the motive behind their work, is to extend the gospel and expand the Kingdom. If they steward that opportunity well, their businesses will grow.

I've been working with pastors, missionaries, and other ministers to shift their mindset on this—to steward the mission in a different way than we've done in the past. Instead of giving our people "fish," we need to give them fishing poles and teach them to fish. In other words, instead of just training them for work and funding it, we need to give them the training to generate their own funding, which will continue to grow and serve them for generations to come.

For example, if we know a pastor in Cuba who has some property and we help them plant fruits and vegetables, that's great. But as ministers, they want to give away everything they grow. The heart behind that is understandable, but the strategy is not good stewardship. So now we're teaching them to divide it up—10 percent to God, 30 percent for themselves and their family, 30 percent to go back into the business, and 30 percent to give away to whomever they want to bless. That's sustainable. The old approach isn't. It's a matter of stewardship.

That requires a shift in thinking, and it applies to any businesstry you want to grow. How do you navigate the issue of what to keep, what to give away, and what to invest for future growth?

Now when we go to Cuba, we ask pastors and leaders to identify people in their congregation who would make good business owners—people who know their identity as sons and daughters of God, understand their why, and are ready to move forward in Kingdom-oriented purposes. We vet them and give them some seed money to get started. We appoint representatives to make sure they're stewarding their finances well, getting a return, and disciplining themselves to distribute their profits to God, their families, the future growth of their business, and the people they just want to bless with their abundance. If we're wise about our stewardship, we can set up perpetual, sustainable Kingdom harvest. That's a good investment.

We've had a lot of pastors and other church leaders in the U.S. tell us they want to do what we're doing with the health-coaching business. They had been relying on one stream of income, which was often just barely sufficient, and when that was significantly reduced because of Covid or some other crisis, they found out they needed some alternatives. Many started getting creative with an online business or some other entrepreneurial adventure, while others were barely able to take care of their families and pay their bills. It brings us back to the question of whether we want to give people fish or give them a fishing pole. Do we want to help people in the moment or coach them on how they can grow a sustainable business that will give them increase? We must steward our opportunities well.

In our business, we're showing a lot of pastors and ministers how they can grow their own income and finance their own Kingdom assignment. We aren't selling anything; we're providing a service. We aren't expecting anything in return; we're giving hope back to people who have tried everything under the sun and haven't found anything that works to get the unwanted weight off *and* keep it off. We're helping people set themselves up for the kind of freedom that enables them to fulfill the calling they've been given without having to wait for two weeks of vacation every year to walk in their destiny.

——— LIVING FROM HEAVEN ———

This requires a complete reorientation in the way we're used to seeing heaven's resources and our access to them.

Many years ago when we lived in New Orleans, we would sometimes go to Mardi Gras parades. Crowds at those parades get thick, and because of all the voices and everything going on, your vision can get skewed and distorted—especially if you're a young child. Our son always had trouble seeing what was going on. He would pull on Ray's pants leg, pleading, "Dad, pick me up! Pick me up!" Ray would pick him up and put him on his shoulders, and he was suddenly able to see everything his father could see.

God wants us to see what He sees. While most people live with an earth-to-heaven orientation, He actually gives us a heaven-to-earth orientation—if we will receive it. We are already seated with Christ in heavenly places (see Ephesians 2:6) and are setting our minds on things above, not on things on earth (see Colossians 3:1-3). Jesus told us to pray "on earth as it is in heaven," meaning our prayers draw from heaven's resources. We live from that vision, seeing ourselves in heavenly places with access to all of heaven's resources, and we position our hearts in that place, literally believing we can have heaven here on earth. No disease, brokenness, or poverty in heaven; no disease, brokenness, or poverty on earth.

> No disease, brokenness, or poverty in heaven; no disease, brokenness, or poverty on earth.

In other words, we don't need to plead for things we already have. Leif often illustrates this with two chairs. In one chair, we're striving, achieving, trying to get what we don't have, living as a servant rather than as a son or daughter. In the other chair, we know who we are and receive what we've been given from a place of rest. We recognize that Jesus is seated at the Father's right hand, in a place of honor, respect, and value, and we're seated there with Him. We can believe God for anything in that place.

For example, our children are part of our family and have access to everything we have. They know that. They don't have to earn their status in the family. That's their identity. But someone who doesn't know their identity in God's family is always trying to earn it, achieve it, strive for it, or validate it. They don't know who they are or whose they are, at least not at a heart level. Without that solid sense of identity, it's easy to live with a poverty mindset and even to equate that poverty with suffering for Jesus. It's a life of trying to pull heaven down *to* where you are rather than calling heaven down *from* where you are. When you have been immersed in a baptism of love and know God as Father, as your heavenly Dad, you live from an entirely different perspective.

God is a good Father and wants to bless His sons and daughters. But we often limit those blessings because our minds aren't trained to believe we can have them. When we pray from earth to heaven, we aren't seeing what our Dad sees. We're trying to figure out what God is doing because we haven't been lifted up to sit on His shoulders. When we know we're seated with Christ in heavenly places—when our heart is positionally there and connected with the rhythm of God's heart—we have a different view, and it's amazing. We start getting ideas and downloads, and doors of opportunity open because we can suddenly see them and enter in.

As I described in chapter 2, toward the end of every year, I ask God for a word for the coming year. In late 2019, I asked Him about 2020, and He said it would be a year of double vision. *Great*, I thought. That sounded cool.

In early 2020, I went to Cuba right as Covid was starting to hit and before everything was locked down. I preached there about the year of double vision, 20/20 vision, and how we would be seeing things in a grander way. An ophthalmologist measures for visual length (distance) and breadth (size), which relates beautifully to seeing what God is doing and how far He is going with it—size and distance. I preached all of this and arrived back in the States wondering why everybody in the airport had masks on. Then everything shut down. And that whole message about vision seemed to be very far off.

"No," God told me, "not if you're seeing things the way I see them, from my Kingdom's perspective." He wanted me to sit on His shoulders and see the bigger picture.

I believe He was saying, "This isn't the way *My* church is supposed to look, how the government of heaven looks, how schools are supposed to teach." In other words, every mountain of society was not functioning the way He mandated them to function, and He was pulling the plug on them for a while. He was putting us in position for a reset. That's a big vision.

In December of that year, I asked God what the word for 2021 would be.

"Double hearing," He said. "There will be a lot of voices out there, and if you don't know the right one, you'll be taken off course."

And it was true. There was a lot going on that year, and anyone listening to the news heard loud, dissonant, confusing voices. Many were listening to the voice of the Dove (peace, comfort, hope), but most were listening to the voice of a pigeon (fear, anxiety, confusion, mistrust).

Then we got to 2022, which God said would be the "year of double blessing." It would be a year of getting heaven's finances to earth. I lived too much of my life from earth to heaven, trying to pull heaven's resources down and hoping we would have enough. But that year marked a shift that I believe is true for the whole church. No more are we to focus on escape, just waiting to get out of here and go to heaven. No, this is an age of getting heaven to earth, and that includes finances as well as every other blessing from heaven. And 2022 was a year of great blessings for Ray and me and many others we know.

It may take time for many to shift their thinking in this area because of what we've long been taught. But this is how sons and daughters of God see with big vision and enter into double blessing. We live from heaven to earth, bringing the abundance of the heavenly realm into our world for the increase of God's kingdom.

—— THE CORE VISION ——

Walking out this calling as priests and kings, learning the rhythm of businesstry, envisioning and stewarding God's resources, and accessing them from our abundant position in heaven rather than our needy position on earth require radical shifts—radical shifts not just in the way we think but also in the way we see: our view of our Father, our identity as His sons and daughters, and our entire understanding of our calling and assignment. It's an adventure, but it might seem like an overwhelming one.

At the most fundamental level, it all comes back to seeking God's Kingdom and His righteousness first and trusting that He will come through with everything else. My life verse, as I mentioned in chapter 2, is Matthew 6:33: "Seek first the kingdom of God and His righteousness, and all these things shall be added to you." God tells us to seek Him and *do what He instructs us to do*—pursue His Kingdom and its righteousness—and He'll take care of everything.

That means that I make sure when I get up every day that God's face is the first thing I look for—not His hand, but His face. He's my priority every day. The rhythm of kingly and priestly life begins there. And in that priority and with that rhythm, doors into hearts and minds will be opened. Nations, cities, and communities can be transformed.

And you, like many other believers in our time, can play a significant part in transforming your world and bringing God's Kingdom into it.

8

Inheritances from Heaven

Many years ago, I was on the Indian Ocean beach in Pemba, Mozambique, with Heidi Baker. It was national Women's Day, and she had brought all the girls and female workers from her ministry's orphanage for a celebration on the shore. She fed them at a beach restaurant and then we all went into the water to play.

With all the joyful shouts and squeals going on around us, Heidi turned to me and said, "We can have so much fun with God!"

She's right. But a lot of believers, and often people in ministry, don't realize that. I didn't either until my baptism of love in 2003. They see God as serious all the time, and they don't realize how much He wants to bless His children and watch them enjoy the gifts He gives. They don't recognize the amazing gift of being able to have fun in His Kingdom.

I've mentioned that building Kingdom wealth is about becoming a channel for God to bless the world through us and advance His Kingdom. That doesn't mean we can't also enjoy those blessings too. We have a nice house and nice cars now, and we don't apologize for that. If I get comments on photos I've posted from the balcony of a hotel room in Punta Cana that judge me for spending money on something other than feeding orphans and growing churches, it's generally from someone who has no idea how much we pour into orphanages, churches, and other ministries. But we know what's most important and are living out our Kingdom priorities. We can build the Kingdom and enjoy it at the same time.

The church's tendency to associate priestly functions and poverty goes back a long way. Many people think Jesus was poor, so the majority of priests live from lack and not abundance. Priests can anoint you, pray for your healing, make sacrifices, and suffer for Jesus, but many are barely getting by. But was Jesus really poor? On one hand, He was born in a stable. On the road, He had no place to lay His head. He certainly wasn't flashy. On the other hand, as we've seen, His earthly father, Joseph, was a businessman who knew how to make money, and Jesus was raised in a business environment. He too was a businessman, a carpenter.

“ We can build the Kingdom and enjoy it at the same time. ”

Scripture tells us that Jesus became poor so that we might become rich (see 2 Corinthians 8:9). Many people automatically read into that, "spiritually rich." But that statement comes in the context of Paul talking about money—actual material wealth and how we are called to give generously. Scripture is full of other references to Jesus sacrificially taking our place in order to lift us up to His.

Jesus took on sin so we might become the righteousness of God in Christ (see 2 Corinthians 5:21). He bore the stripes of a whip so we could be healed (see Isaiah 53:5, another passage with huge spiritual implications, though Matthew 8:17 applies it to physical healing). He was forsaken by His Father so we could be adopted as sons and daughters (see Matthew 27:46; Romans 8:15-17; Ephesians 1:5). So if Jesus was stripped of the blessings of heaven and earth so that we could have them in all these other ways, would that not also include some measure of financial abundance? The divine exchange on the cross was comprehensive. But we have historically been so afraid of the abuses of a "gospel of wealth" or "prosperity teaching" that we've gone completely the other way and left financial provision out of the picture.

We need to be comfortable hanging out both with people in the dirt and with people in the palace. Like Paul, we need to know how to be content in every situation, whether in plenty or in want (see Philippians 4:12). No matter how much we instinctively emphasize the "want," the balance also includes the "plenty."

The last time I went to Cuba, I was able to take $5,000 with me to buy rice and beans for a huge number of people, and I didn't have to check my checkbook to do it. A baked chicken costs $65 there as I'm writing this, and most people are making hardly any money. It feels good to be able to feed a lot of people and let them know it comes from a God who loves them and wants to bless them. If I want to put on a banquet for Muslim women in Pakistan so they can hear the Good News and build relationships with Christian women, I don't have to spend weeks or months raising money for that. I've done that before, and there's nothing wrong with it, but now I can just plan something whenever I need to.

Kingdom wealth is an enormous, strategic asset for Kingdom purposes.

──── NO POVERTY IN HEAVEN ────

We know amazing people who have served in other countries for years. They've received good financial support. Like any of us, they have the opportunity to start a business that would generate good income and perhaps allow them to depend less on fundraising. There's nothing wrong with raising financial support; that's often how God provides for those serving Him. But if we're entering into a new season of Kingdom finances, as I and many other well-known ministers believe we are, maybe it's time to think about additional ways of funding Kingdom work.

We know missionaries who have preached that if there is no cancer, no disease, no infirmity in heaven, then there should be none on earth. They are great at carrying and preaching the message of "on earth as it is in heaven," and they have seen miraculous healings through their ministry. But I've been told they believe their riches are stored up for them in heaven and not on earth.

We do have riches stored up for us in heaven. That's true. But I'd challenge them with some questions: Is there poverty in heaven? Any lack or financial need? And if there isn't, should we just accept financial need on earth—for ourselves or anyone else? If we base healing on the fact that there's no disease in heaven, shouldn't we also base our supply on the fact that there's no poverty in heaven?

God is raising up entrepreneurs and businesstries in order to fund their Kingdom assignments. That doesn't mean the age of raising financial support for mission work has come to an end, but it may not be the primary means of support going forward. If God is equipping His people to build Kingdom wealth, we can do a lot of Kingdom work through the revenue that comes from it in addition to what generous givers are supporting. We need it all.

Those are the lenses we look through, whether it's finances, relationships, health, or anything else. We believe in "on earth as it is in heaven," and just as there is no cancer, heart disease, paralysis, broken relationships, obesity, or any other evidence of the fall in heaven, neither is there any financial lack in heaven.

We have a different kind of *riches* waiting for us in heaven. We won't need money there. But we do need financial sufficiency here on earth in this generation and the generations to come. And I think people who serve God in any capacity, in any field, need to shift their thinking. There may be seasons in our lives when financial wellbeing is a challenge, but God wants more for us than just eking out a living and stretching every penny as if He is short on resources. He wants us to walk in an abundance mindset so we can advance His Kingdom abundantly on earth.

Discerning Christians have been conditioned to contrast austere or modest living with "the gospel of wealth," as though any association of the gospel with wealth simply means getting rich for self-serving purposes. But there's a big difference between wanting to get rich in order to be rich and building wealth in order to fund Kingdom work. All Kingdom work in every period of history has been funded by people who have money. We often say in our business, "Money in the hands of good people will do great things!"

Sure, there are people abusing the gift of financial blessings. But there are people abusing every other gift God can give us too, and we don't throw the gifts out just because of the abuses. Many people are abusing food, but we don't stop eating or call food evil. People try to spend counterfeit money, but we don't get rid of all our cash. We don't let the misuse of other gifts keep us from enjoying them in the right way.

> " Many people are abusing food, but we don't
> stop eating or call food evil. "

I hear people talking all the time about Kingdom work they would like to do—opening a home for women and children who are victims of human trafficking, feeding orphans, going on a mission trip, helping build a church or reach a country with the gospel. "Why don't you do it?" I ask.

"Because I don't have the money" is almost always part of the answer.

They sense God calling them, but they don't have the means to answer the call. But money is not God's problem. Why are we being held back because of finances when God is the one who owns it all? As His sons and daughters, we just need to know how to access it.

This does not begin with the wallet or pocketbook. It's not about just getting another job or starting a random business. There's some strategy to it. But the first place that strategy begins is in the mind and the heart. For us, it was assuming we were serving Jesus best by driving rundown cars and rationing the care packages we were given. We had to learn to think and feel differently about money and wealth. That's where the shift needs to happen first.

The next step is learning how to dream. If you want to become a channel for God's blessings to the world, dream of how you would like to do that. You can't do that until you let go of some judgments you may have made in the past. Many Christians have looked at people of wealth with condemnation or contempt, as if they are all living selfishly. There seems to be a temptation to roll their eyes and swear off any desire to ever be a millionaire, as if becoming one is inherently unrighteous.

Do you know how much wealthy people give and to which causes? Do you know the sacrifices they have made? Do you assume they were handed everything and never had to work for it? Have you considered that they might be the source of funding for numerous missionaries and charities around the world—and that this may be an important part of their calling and a God-given Kingdom assignment? We can't know all the answers to those questions—we don't get an inside view of everybody's lives—yet many people feel the freedom to judge anyway. If that has been a tendency for you, be careful there. You may be cursing your own future assignment by your words, actions, or thoughts.

I would encourage you to let go of all those assumptions, if you have them, and learn to see wealth as a Kingdom opportunity. Then let yourself dream. Bring your dreams into your conversations with your extravagant, generous Father. See what direction they go in and how He leads. You may be surprised at where He takes you.

We are all called to invest ourselves in the Kingdom of God. In whatever areas you experience increase—in wisdom, love, commitment, and yes, finances—you have more of yourself to give. Seeing life through Kingdom lenses means looking at people, communities, cities, nations, and entire cultures that need God. We begin to see them as an inheritance to be received from the God who holds all power and resources in His hands.

―――― HEIRS TO NATIONS AND BUSINESSES ――――

Several years ago, I was facing up to five years in prison. Our ministry in Cuba was supporting about twenty pastors at $25 a month. Pastors there were generally at the bottom of the social scale, often making about $15 a month, so this was a good investment in them. I'd taken people on trips there for years and had places on my website where people could sponsor pastors and churches.

When I was at the African Call in Tanzania in 2008, one of my spiritual sons from Cuba messaged me to say we needed to talk as soon as I got home. That was going to be in two weeks, but he said he would wait. Finally, when I got home, I called and asked what was going on.

> " Several years ago, I was facing up to five years in prison. "

"I think there's trouble, Mom," he told me. He said a pastor from New York was in Cuba, and my spiritual son had walked into a room where this pastor had printouts of my website laid out on a table. Sure enough, the next Monday morning I got a letter from the U.S. Department of the

Treasury. I was looking at a lot of potential fines and the possibility of five years imprisonment for sponsoring pastors in Cuba.

As I mentioned earlier, God had told me in 2006 that He would give me Cuba as an inheritance. It was the last night of a conference, and I was on the floor, wrecked with God's presence and just soaking Him in. "God," I said, "just as you gave Mozambique to Heidi Baker, I want Cuba."

"It's yours, my daughter," He said. "Take it."

So I reached my hands into heaven and put Cuba in my heart. How? I don't know how it works. I just did. How does a brown cow eat green grass and produce white milk? I don't have to know how it happens to enjoy a glass of cold milk with hot chocolate chip cookies. It tastes amazing! I don't look at that milk and try to figure out the process. I just drink it down. I don't know how I had received Cuba, but I knew I did.

Psalm 2:8 says, "Ask of Me, and I will give You the nations for Your inheritance, and the ends of the earth for Your possession." The verse before that is addressed to the Son. I realized after my baptism of love that I had been working for nations rather than receiving them, but we inherit nations as sons and daughters, not as servants or slaves. Even when read as a messianic psalm inviting God's Son to ask for the nations of the world (see verse 7), it still applies. We are Jesus' coheirs. We inherit what He inherits, and I had asked for Cuba as my share.

I came home from that trip and wondered, *How far will I go for this nation that I had just received as an inheritance?*

I ordered Brother Andrew's book *God's Smuggler* and devoured it. After that, I knew I was willing to give my life for Cuba. I still would today. I knew God had led me to do what I was doing in sponsoring pastors there, and if going to prison would give me a voice for the suffering church in that nation, I would humbly go. I just didn't know what to make of this sudden opposition to it.

This inquiry from the authorities came while I was working for Leif. He was traveling out of the country with his son. I asked Mama Jen Hetland if they had an attorney. I contacted my ministry board and the pastor of our church in Iowa, who was an advisor on my board. My license for working in Cuba was under that church at the time, and I made it clear that I did not want this to reflect on the church or the board. I urged them to distance themselves from me. Instead, they promised to stick with me no matter what.

We met with our kids, who had been raised in Mexico, been held at gunpoint in the deserts in Mexico, and witnessed the effects of bombs going off in El Salvador during its civil war. They had been around these interesting, faith-building scenarios enough not to be surprised. Their response was, "Mom, we know you'd do anything crazy for God!"

Finally, I was able to talk to Leif by phone, and he asked me how I was doing. "Well, if I keep the lenses of the Kingdom in front of my eyes, I'm actually doing well. If they begin to slide down and I look through natural lenses, I get a little nervous." I knew I was a little fish in a small pond—I wasn't a threat to the country like some terrorist, and my work wasn't widespread enough to get much attention, even in the context of the U.S. embargo of Cuba at that time—so someone must have turned me in. I had been singled out.

The U.S. government gave me thirty days to pull my response together, so we gathered what they needed and sent it to them. In the meantime, I flew to Iowa to meet with my board and tell them that I wanted to release them because I wasn't sure where this was headed. I told them I would not hold anything against them or be upset with them if any of them stepped off the board. They had all been on a trip to one nation or another with me, and they all said they were staying and had my back.

Not long afterward, our pastor in Iowa called me to say the FBI had just shown up at the church unannounced. They wanted to know how he knew me—we had known each other for sixteen years—and what my relationship with the church was, and they had many other questions. Our pastor told them the truth about everything.

We received a form in the mail a few days later wanting additional information, and we filled it out and sent it back. We haven't heard anything since. I still count Cuba as my inheritance.

I believe we also receive businesses as an inheritance like we can receive nations. Inheritance is a very biblical concept. As Kingdom people doing Kingdom work, we have every right as God's sons and daughters to ask Him for inheritances He has promised to give.

I'm very aware that there is opposition to this message. That's fine; I'm used to opposition. Before moving to Ohio, I got letters telling me not to come because, as a female pastor, I wasn't wanted there. For the first ten months of my time there, a group of men (not from our church) would meet every other Sunday to figure out how to run me out of town, like they didn't have anything better to do on a Sunday afternoon. I was called a cult leader and a Muslim pastor (I haven't figured that one out yet), but I knew I was on a Kingdom assignment to shift a culture in a church and a community. It stung, of course, but I didn't lose any sleep over it because I knew God had put me there for His Kingdom assignment.

So I'm not surprised when people question the concept of a "missionary millionaire." What they don't know is how much ministry we accomplish with the resources God has blessed us with. We'd been generous; now we could give extravagantly. We've helped family members with many of their needs. We've grown an inheritance that we can leave to our children, grandchildren, and great-grandchildren. We've poured into churches and orphanages and the lives of pastors and missionaries. We know we're on assignment to shift the thinking of people to understand the gospel of the Kingdom—to realize we can do a better job of expanding the Kingdom and fulfilling the Great Commission if we have greater resources to do it.

Again, God's not short on funding. We just must learn how to access what He wants to give and have hearts and minds that have been tested and can be trusted to steward it well.

We still live by faith. We always plan our giving in a way that we know will stretch us. But we can do a lot of things that used to stretch us and don't anymore. I can invest in events in Cuba or Pakistan or wherever without sweating over the checkbook balance to see if they are doable. Financial freedom includes the freedom to pick up and go to Cuba for a couple of weeks and support the ministry there if I need to, or fund something big to reach women behind the veil.

—— A CHANNEL OF BLESSING ——

Once on a trip to Pakistan, I led an outdoor women's event that went very well. A lot of women encountered God. The next day was Mother's Day in the U.S., but I didn't think it was celebrated there, so I wondered on our first day in the country why I kept seeing signs everywhere in Urdu, the Pakistani language, with the word "women" in English on them. So I asked Robert, one of our leaders there, what all those signs were saying.

"The government declared this to be Women's Week," he explained. "It's the first time in Pakistani history."

I almost fell out of my seat. Here, in a Muslim country and culture, women were being honored. I had been to Pakistan many times and had never seen or heard anything like this.

We had a dinner planned a couple of nights later—coinciding with Mother's Day in the U.S., and now, as I found out, with Women's Week in Pakistan. It was for thirty leading Christian women and thirty leading Muslim women who were scholars from the university where Leif had spoken a few days before. (Speaking to an audience that included women was kind of unheard of, but doors like that seem to open for Leif all the time.) Our church back home had gathered some gifts for these women—scarves and jewelry—that they anointed, prayed over, and put in gift bags.

I rented out a restaurant, ordered the best food, and had some long tables set up. The Christian women came to sit by me, but I told them to spread out. They would sit on one side of the tables, and their Muslim sisters would sit across from them so they could do life together for a couple of hours. Many of the Christian women had met before, but none of the Muslim women had, so I greeted all of them as they came in and took their seats.

"I want to thank you all for coming," I began. "This is such an honor. Tomorrow in the U.S. we honor all the mothers in our country, and I know most of you here are mothers too, so I want to honor you tonight. We are all created in God's image, and He wants to know all of you as His beautiful daughters. So let's just break bread and enjoy life together this evening."

I just wanted to win their hearts, not focus on evangelism and getting a decision from them. With that approach, they would have cut me off, left, and never come back. But they knew I did not have a hook. Like Esther, a Jew winning the heart of a Persian king; like Daniel, shifting the king's heart; like Joseph, demonstrating that he cared about the welfare of a country foreign to him, I wanted them to know they were loved and honored.

> " With that approach, they would have cut me off,
> left, and never come back. "

When the dinner was done, we gave them their gifts. By the end of those two hours, those Muslim women wanted selfies with me and asked when I was coming back. They posted it all on their Facebook pages. I was told nothing like that had been done in Pakistan before, where Christian and Muslim women came together for dinner. I paid $6,000 for the event the night before and for that dinner—part of it for the protection of guards holding AK-47s to protect us—but it was worth much more than that.

Leif asked me what I wanted to do the next time. "They've still been asking for you to come back," he said.

I told him I wanted to up it—two hundred women instead of sixty. It would cost a lot more, but it would be such a great investment for the Kingdom. I wouldn't be wrong to let other people invest in that type of event, but my point is that I don't need to wait around and take time away from our business to try to raise money. I'll have no worries about whether it will come together, no anxiety about where the money will come from. I know I could just write the check.

That said, there are many people who sow into our ministry consistently, and I'm very thankful for that. Most of those people are not in a position to go to the places I go, and since they can't, they partner to send me, almost always based on our relationship with them.

Similarly, we almost always sow into other people's ministries out of relationship. Because of the huge business we have grown, many people contact us to ask for money for some mission trip or other Kingdom assignment. Though Ray and I love to bless Kingdom work, we never want it to be because someone learned that we have money and assume we're a source of provision for them. We do support many ministries and missionaries, but always based on relationship and not simply the fact that we have money. When a hurricane blew through south Florida recently, many organizations needed help, but we chose one that we knew about and trusted. We sow financially where Kingdom relationships have been established.

I love funding ministry events like I did in Pakistan. I love blessing people there, in Sri Lanka, or wherever else God leads. He has recently narrowed my focus back to Cuba and promised to take care of our business—to bring it to a whole new level, in fact—if I'll take care of His people there. And I can. I have the freedom to do that because of a yes a few years ago and a willingness to invest in God's purposes in my life, my family's life, and His Kingdom.

Joyce Meyer got this right many years ago. She nailed our "stinkin thinkin" about finances. She took a lot of heat for that—anyone who becomes a minister of Kingdom wealth is going to get grilled by people who don't get it—and I know I may get some of that too. But I know my assignments. I love pouring abundance into the nations and my family. I love being able to sit with people at a restaurant and pick up the check without fretting about whether I have enough to cover it. I can just bless people the way I want to bless them.

And just as the Bible says it's more blessed to give than to receive (see Acts 20:35), I always feel like I'm the one who gets the bigger blessing.

9

Living in Your Why

When I first reached the $6,000 a month mark in nine months of our health-coaching business, I was talking with my sponsoring coach on the phone. She has known our family for years, including our kids and grandkids. She had been with me to Cuba and Mexico and served in women's conferences with me.

"Leanne, you know this business is willable, right?" she asked me.

"What do you mean it's 'willable'?"

"I mean you can pass this on to Beth and Jeff and their families."

I've always taught about knowing your why. You have to know why you're doing what you do and be motivated by it so that you'll know what to say yes to and what to say no to. When I speak at conferences and conventions, I encourage people to have layered whys—multiple levels that help you prioritize and keep your focus on what's most important. When you have a big enough why, you'll do whatever you have to do.

By "layered whys," I mean figuring out your next goal, looking for your next reason for the season—the next Kingdom dream. For example, my first why with our coaching business was seeing the people who had had great success with it and thinking I and everyone else on the planet has the right to look like them. Then nine months later, I found out I was a FIBC, a Fully Integrated Business Coach. Helping others reach that goal was another layer of why. Then I found out the business was willable; we could pass it on to our children and grandchildren—further build the inheritance I was leaving them and our grandchildren. That was my next why.

Fast-forward a couple of years, and we ended up with a million-dollar-a-month business. As I mentioned, it took me a little while to figure out exactly what that meant—that a million dollars' worth of health resources was being processed through our business *every single month*. And our account just kept growing.

When we found out we had reached millionaire status, a couple who is part of our mentorship team told us, "This is so exciting! When we hit millionaire, our goal was to help ten more people become millionaires, and you and Ray are our tenth!" That meant more to me than the bonus that came with it. Someone who hadn't known us before we stepped into this business had been dreaming about us even before they knew our names. They had previously shared with us that they were executive pastors for twenty-seven years. Now he is a minister and an entrepreneur. Instead of living paycheck to paycheck, barely able to pay the bills, he had now gotten to the point of earning a significant monthly income.

"We saw where this was heading for us," they explained. "We recognized what it could bring us in terms of Kingdom wealth and ministry capacity. We knew we would be able to fund a lot of things that had only been distant hopes and dreams before."

Ray and I wanted to do what they had done too in helping at least ten people get to this point. That became our next layered why—to help at least ten people become millionaires too.

God had spoken to me after I started coaching. "Leanne, I gave you the program for your health, but I gave you the business for your finances so you can go where you want to go, do what you want to do, and give to whomever you want to give. Money will never be a question, so don't ask me for it again."

> ❝ Money will never be a question, so don't ask me for it again. ❞

We haven't had to. We can fund our own assignments. We can go anywhere in the world, feed any orphans we want to feed, fund a church in Cuba, throw a banquet for Muslim women in Pakistan so they can experience true honor and God's love and see how His Kingdom operates, and bless any ministry and any person we want to bless. We're fulfilling dreams that at one time were just wishes, and most wishes don't come true.

Those whys give us vision. They drive us forward.

Most people just sit around and hope something happens—in our work, the equivalent of hoping someone just comes and knocks on our door, says they want to be part of our team, and asks for help building a business. That's not how it works. We must live out loud on social media, and not on separate pages that compartmentalize our roles. I'm a wife, mother, grandmother, pastor, author, speaker, and health coach on one encompassing Facebook page. The same goes for other social media sources. I don't hide anything. It's all out there because people want authenticity and vulnerability, not some page or presentation that looks like you're trying to hook them or sell them something.

My first why has always been people. I do what I do to help people—not to get more or move higher, though that often happens when you're doing what you're called to do. But I work very hard to make sure my vision remains focused on meeting the needs of people. That didn't stop when this business started to grow. I decided that I wouldn't sell, push, or try to manipulate a client or hook a coach. I was going to do this only because I thought people needed what the business offered for their health, their finances, and their overall lives and future.

When my coach told me this business could be passed down to my kids and grandkids, that became our next why. It meant we would be able to leave more than just a legacy for them. We could leave an inheritance.

We've been in full-time ministry since 1984 and didn't have anything to leave our children. We didn't have a retirement account, and even though we knew we'd get Social Security, we certainly weren't expecting that to pay our bills—not even living at the level we had gotten used to as missionaries. Ray had a small inheritance, but we had cashed that in a long time ago. We were trusting God for our future. But we also really wanted to leave something to our kids and grandkids.

Those are the kinds of whys that keep us going. And they've blessed our lives and the lives of many, many others.

—— YOUR DREAM AND YOUR WHY ——

I led a school on leadership in Iowa that began when we were living in Nashville. Much of our focus was on shifting from that mindset of living out only a priestly anointing to stepping into a kingly anointing too. One of the requirements was to read one book a month and write a report on it, and one of the books I assigned was by one of our mentoring coaches: *Church Boy to Millionaire* by Doug Wood. Doug owned a furniture store for years but was overweight and generally unhealthy and going through hard times to the point of filing for bankruptcy. It was a terrible situation.

Now Doug is one of the top coaches in our company and makes seven figures a month. The cover of the book shows him wearing a beautiful suit and sitting in a leather chair.

He's the one who coined the term "businesstry." Some of my students weren't sure what to think of the book at first. One student thought, *What's this guy in that nice suit and leather chair going to try to sell me?* But once they got into it, they were captivated. One report was by a woman who needed to lose about eighty pounds, and she wrote that her spirit tuned in when Doug was talking about being an entrepreneur. She said she knew that ran in her family's veins, and she wanted to do that because she thought she'd love it.

I texted this student to tell her I'd been reading her report and wanted to talk to her. She told her husband I'd texted and wanted to talk. She thought she must have done something wrong, but we got on a video call a couple of days later and I explained. (If you're ready to grow your own business/businesstry and be an entrepreneur, Ray and I can help you as well.)

"I saw what you wrote in your report, and I know you want to be an entrepreneur. I've got a business for you."

After we talked through it for a while, she said she wanted to do it. She became a client and a coach at the same time, and before she even started the program, she had sponsored three people. Her mindset had shifted already. She didn't worry about what people on Facebook might think or have any concern that she would come across as trying to sell something. She had a gift to give away, and she went after it. She had a goal for her family, a big why that moved her forward without hesitation. She's done amazing as a health coach on our team, *and* she's lost those eighty-plus pounds and has learned how to keep it off for life.

> " Her mindset had shifted already. "

Most people don't get where they want to go because they don't have a why. We get coaches to join us because they are motivated by a why. They know what they want. Some of them have incredible stories. One was a dental hygienist for twenty-four years. She was able to replace her income in six months of coaching. She has five kids, and one was born with the umbilical cord around his neck. Doctors told her he would never talk or be able to go to school, but he has; he recently graduated from high school. They are now putting him in a school that will teach him how to talk. It costs $4,000 a month. It never would have happened if she hadn't acted on her why. She is now one of the top coaches in our organization.

A lot of people look at these people from the outside and think they're just out to make money—that wealth is their why. We live in a very judgmental society—even within the church, I'm sorry to say—in which people don't understand the story behind what they see but feel the freedom to pass judgment on it anyway. This former dental hygienist's why included a very real need for her child to be cared for if something happened to her and her husband. Her business grew supernaturally fast because everyone who came within five feet of her learned how she lost a hundred pounds. God gave her solutions to the whys that drive her.

Most people don't understand the power of what finances can do for their family, church, community, or nation. They think in terms of addition instead of multiplication, and because addition can be so slow, they grow discouraged. Their thinking is limited. So, one thing I do when I'm talking with a potential coach is what we call a "dream assessment." I get on a video call with them and step into their lives and their dreams.

First I'll ask them to tell me about their lives—how many kids, single parent or couple, job situation, and so on. If I'm talking with a single mom trying to take care of two kids while balancing three jobs, I'm not going to ask, "What would another $25,000 a month do for you?" Mentally she couldn't get there. But another one or two thousand a month? That's a conceivable amount of extra money that would help stoke those dreams. She could quit one of her jobs. I tell her we can help her accomplish that.

At the other end of the spectrum, I did a dream assessment with a nurse practitioner whose husband was a critical care nurse. On the video call, I could tell they lived in a comfortable home. So, I asked her, "If money wasn't a factor, what would you do that you can't do now?" Everybody has a bucket list, right? Whether it's to climb Mount Kilimanjaro, send their child to a special school, or transform a nation. Hers was to take a six-month cruise that would cost around $40,000.

"I could pay for that in one month," I told her. That piqued her interest in a hurry.

"Let's do it!" she blurted. She got on board and today is building a phenomenal business. She is also helping a lot of people at the hospital she works at lose weight and get healthy. Go figure—a health coach getting a health-care community healthy! Her husband just retired from being a critical care nurse. They are finally able to do many of the things God has put on their hearts to do.

> " "I could pay for that in one month," I told her.
> That piqued her interest in a hurry. "

We're living in tumultuous economic times. People need extra money. More than two-thirds of Americans live paycheck to paycheck and have less than $1,000 in their bank account, according to pre-Covid stats. Those statistics are even higher now. There are many opportunities out there that people are not tapping into because they don't see the possibilities, are trapped in limiting ways of thinking, or are afraid of taking the next step.

Those figures include many in the church. There are several reasons people aren't flocking to our church doors, and one of them is that many of us live paycheck to paycheck and file for bankruptcy. They look at lifestyles that don't line up with our teaching and beliefs and reject any thought of learning from us. As a pastor, I stayed awake at night wondering why people out there wouldn't want what we have. Why weren't they knocking down our doors? Among other reasons, most Christians don't know how to hang out with kings and honor those who are blessed financially and are always asking for money.

We're on a mission to get the church and the world healthy not only in spirit, mind, and body but also in finances because money is a huge stress factor that affects health, relationships, and lifestyles. Financial stress contributes to weight gain and divorce. Most people are so practiced in putting restraints around their vision that they don't know how to hope or dream anymore. They've resigned themselves to the *status quo* or the slow, arduous climb out of it. When I do a dream assessment, we address all of that.

Notice that this is all about asking questions. In the evangelical world, we've been heavy on giving information, even before getting to know the person we're talking to. We're all about "tell, tell, tell." But when we get to know people and build a relationship with them, we don't have to focus on telling and selling. We encourage, coach, challenge, and walk with them into their upgrade, and lives change.

That's a big why. This is what it's all about. The Kingdom advances rapidly the more people step into their God-given dreams and destinies.

I received a "dream award" for stirring up dreams in people a couple of years ago. I had no idea I was even up for it, but at an event in Phoenix, one of my spiritual daughters from Atlanta told me she had nominated me for it. Out of several hundred coaches in the room, fifteen or twenty would get one of these awards, so I wasn't expecting it. But when the emcee said, "This person grew her business half the time from Cuba," I broke down crying. I love pulling dreams out of people and seeing them step out of their self-imposed limitations, whether it's in Cuba, personal relationships, or coaches in our organization.

I also love making the church more beautiful—full of hope and expectation, love and honor, generosity, and blessing. I love building the Kingdom in all of its aspects.

—— DIGGING YOUR WELLS OF HOPE ——

Once people have a dream—when they know their why—the next big question is how to move toward it. People want to get from point A to point B. But it isn't always just a matter of taking the right steps or following a particular action plan. That may be part of it, but even before you get there, it involves opening yourself up to what your Father wants to do and noticing the opportunities He puts in front of you.

For example, we weren't looking to start a business, though it was a dream in the recesses of our hearts and minds. It wasn't even on our radar. It was something God brought into our lives through relationships and circumstances as we were carrying out our assignment and minding our own business.

I have a whole message I preach about what happens when you're minding your own business and you're in alignment with the Kingdom of God. Gideon was beating out the sheaves in a winepress when the angel appeared and told him to deliver Israel from the Philistines. Saul was looking for his father's lost sheep when Samuel found him and told him he would be Israel's first king. Elisha was plowing his fields when Elijah threw his mantle over him and picked him to carry on the prophet's assignment. Whatever Mary was doing when Gabriel announced she would give birth to God, she certainly wasn't expecting that. They were all minding their own business when God stepped in with His big Kingdom plans.

If you're in alignment with the Kingdom of God—if you're a Matthew 6:33 person who is seeking His Kingdom and His righteousness first—God will step into your days at unanticipated moments and lead you into your next Kingdom assignment, whatever that happens to be. That doesn't mean you should be completely passive—you'll need to keep your eyes open and pursue your Kingdom dreams to whatever degree you can—but God very often shows up when you're minding your own business.

I had a lot of business ideas over the years. I'd started working when I was 15 because if the kids in our family wanted anything extra, we had to get it on our own. We've done a lot of things over the years, but nothing ever seemed like it was "the thing." The one that really took off in recent years was the one we weren't even looking for. We never anticipated having a multimillion-dollar business with no overhead and couldn't have planned it if we tried.

I think a lot of people in ministry would love to have their own business because they know what it's like selling plasma to get by. Many have opted out of Social Security, have no retirement plan, and are starting to wonder how it's all going to work out for them. They are looking down the road and thinking an extra source of income might really be useful. They also know that many of their dreams depend on funding that they don't currently have and don't know how to get. I recently had a minister tell me that he can only hope one of his five children love him and his wife enough to take care of them as they age, as they have no retirement account and know very well that Social Security will not take care of their bills.

Sometimes it's much easier to dream for other people than for ourselves. I spent much of my life trying to help other people walk in their God-given destiny—I even got that "dream award" for helping others unlock their dreams—but eventually realized I had trouble figuring out my own dreams. It wasn't something I had really thought about. I've always been able to envision all kinds of ministry opportunities and goals, which obviously I've had a huge stake in. Those were my dreams too. But in terms of unlocking personal dreams that God wanted to fulfill for me? That was another story. That needed to shift, and it did! God is the greatest dreamer, and He has taught me how to dream.

There's nothing wrong with enjoying what God has given us. Being poor and suffering are not spiritual obligations. We do need to know how to suffer; if Jesus hadn't suffered, He would not have been able to identify with those who do. We need that experience and that capacity too. But that's not the same as embracing lifelong poverty and suffering for their own sake as a spiritual virtue. Again, we have to know how to hang out both with the poor *and* with kings. We are supposed to feel comfortable in both realms.

"God is the greatest dreamer, and He has taught me how to dream."

My first two years working in Cuba, I went every four to six weeks just to help them cultivate this idea of dreaming—digging those wells of hope. I suggested that we hold a pastors' conference and was told, "We can't do that here."

"Why not?" I asked. I understood that they lived under a lot of restrictions and oppression, but I also knew the God who lives above them.

"You don't understand," they said. "We just can't do that."

I finally convinced them that we could.

Then they said, "Okay, we'll invite twenty-five pastors from across the island."

Well, I knew that wasn't a multiplication factor for transformation. The Kingdom of God is about multiplication, not addition. "No, let's do 100 pastors," I replied.

"What? How are we going to pay for that, with all the accommodations, food, transportation, and everything else?" At that time, pastors were making about $15 a month and would never be able to afford to travel across the country for a three-day event.

"Don't worry about the finances. I'll take care of that," I assured them.

So we did our first three-day pastors' conference. It was amazing! Pastors from across the country attended, and as a result the Kingdom of God is exponentially advancing in

Cuba. Our network now oversees 350 churches in that beautiful nation.

Since that first event in 2006, their entire perspective has changed. "Guess what, Mom?" they said to me a couple of years later. "We had a youth conference and paid for it ourselves. We had youth from all over the country!"

They had learned how to dream—and not just to dream wishfully but to take steps of faith toward their dreams. Now when I go to Cuba, I'm able to have some Cuban coffee with them, sit in a rocking chair for a time, and watch these sons and daughters do what they once thought impossible.

When we just show up as priests, hoping it all works out, praying and fasting and crossing our fingers that we'll be able to pay for it, we have given in to a limited perspective that doesn't take in the whole of Kingdom living. My mind has completely shifted from that approach over the years. There is so much more we can do. And there are so many more whys to keep us moving toward it.

Conclusion

In the words of my friend Matt Sorger, God is breaking the mold. He is bringing His people out of those false assumptions that the work of ministry is done by ministers and supported by businesspeople, and that lacking resources is somehow spiritual. God wants to prosper all His people. He wants to make many ministers into businesspeople and many businesspeople into ministers because the work of ministry is done by all and financed by all. He is erasing and removing those divisions and limitations we have placed on ourselves. He wants to bless us as conduits of His Kingdom so we can help transform the world.

In order to do that, we need to step out of the boat and onto the waves, just like Peter did when Jesus called him out in a storm. We all find ourselves in storms from time to time. Peter did as well. But he didn't just step out in the midst of a storm; he tried walking in it too. People jump out of boats into the water every day. Anyone can do that. But the miracle is walking on water after leaving the boat! That means leaving the familiar for the unfamiliar, just as I and others who have shared their stories in this book have done. He wants His people to put behind their misunderstandings about blessing and abundance in our spirits, souls, bodies, and finances, and to embrace new ways and take new steps of faith into the greater blessings He has planned for us.

Hear God's invitation to step out of the old and into the new. He is calling you to dig wells of hope in your life and the lives of others. He is inviting you to shift the way you think and get comfortable in the realms of priests *and* kings. He has already positioned you in heavenly places with heaven's authority, and He has filled your life with a multitude of whys that will pull you toward your destiny. And He has promised to set you up for that destiny by opening doors and walking through them with you—maybe even while you are just minding your own business.

In other words, you have everything you need for this journey. The next step of it begins today.

THE

TRANSFORMATIONAL COACH

MINISTRY CONTACT INFORMATION:

info@leannegoffministries.org
www.facebook.com/LeanneGoffMinistries
www.linkedin.com/in/leannegoffministries
https://www.instagram.com/leannegoffministries/

For more information on inviting Leanne to speak,
upcoming conferences, International Vision Trips,
or to purchase items from our web store,
please visit our website at:

www.leannegoffministries.org

LGM INTERNATIONAL VISION TRIPS

LGM Vision Trips are the experience of a lifetime.
The purpose of our International Vision Trips
is to proclaim the salvation of the Kingdom,
the love of the Father, and demonstrate signs,
wonders, and miracles to those desperately in need
of a revelation of their identities as sons and daughters of God.

Are YOU ready for a Kingdom Family adventure?

go to

http://www.leannegoffministries.org/visiontrips

MORE FROM LEANNE GOFF

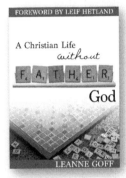

Also available in Spanish

A CHRISTIAN LIFE WITHOUT FATHER GOD

We really do not know God, as He desires to be known, until we know Him as Father. When we begin to see the centrality of this truth in the Bible, we hold a new book in our hands. Leanne walks us through the most painful seasons of her life. She came out not only a presentation of what it means to call God "Father," but she has also come into a powerful alignment with the Kingdom of God: the Family Business. She has become her message, pointing to a path made clear, on how to become a son or daughter of God.

BREAKING THE VEIL OF SILENCE

Why were you born? What is your God Designed Destiny? This book contains 15 stories of ones who have broken through the "Veil of Silence" and are now walking out their Designed Destiny as Father God's mature sons and daughters. Each story will inspire you to maturity as His son or daughter. They also contain a prayer and/or declaration to you the reader that will encourage you to break through the veil of shame, guilt, embarrassment, generational curses, etc. that have kept you silent far too long!

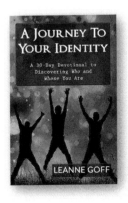

A JOURNEY TO YOUR IDENTITY

Leanne uses the introduction of this message by Leif Hetland, her spiritual father, as a springboard to show us the value and importance of leaning our hearts into the heart of Father God, as well as spiritual fathers and mothers. When we lean back into their hearts and come into alignment, we will receive the secrets of the Kingdom, as John the Beloved did, and go forth in our assignment and fulfill our destiny.